Praise for *He S[...]*

MW00835118

"I've known Diane and her husband Phil for years—since their first date, actually. It was before marriage, before kids, and before her deafness set in. I have had the privilege and joy of watching her story play out and seeing God work in the midst. I have seen her live through the confusion and challenges of her deafness, digging deep into the inevitable questions it brings. She sees it as a story of failure. I see it as a story of triumphant faith. Trusting God in a storm is seldom simple and clean. More often than not, faith is messy, full of bumps and valleys and questions and heartache. And for Diane, her faith and relationship with her Creator has been shrouded in physical silence. I challenge you to read her story and not be moved. I have no doubt that her story will cause you to rethink your own understanding of God."

—*Luis Palau,* world evangelist and author

"Diane Comer captivates the reader as she describes in profound ways her sudden world of silence. Her prose is poetic. In a riveting manner, she tells of her journey from a normal life that heard chirping birds, falling rain, a baby's coo, and a lover's whisper to one of silence. She went from hearing laughter among her girlfriends, the singing of her husband, and her child calling "Mom" to a world on mute. Few of us ever think about the reality of absolute deafness, but Diane narrates so powerfully that we enter her soundless world. When she cries, we cry. When she doubts, we doubt. When her faith ignites, our faith ignites. Amazingly, along with her, we hear God in the silence. What did God say? *He Speaks in the Silence* answers that question. Oh, and find out why, when she regained her hearing through the miracle of science, she daily disconnects to reenter her world of silence."

—*Emerson and Sarah Eggerichs* of Love and Respect Ministries, author of *Love and Respect*

If you have ever wondered (as most of us do) ... Does God see me? Does he want to talk to me? Is it possible for me to hear him speak? Diane's story, compellingly and beautifully told, gets to the nitty gritty reality of what it means to know God deeply and intimately in all the silence *and* the noise of life's good days, hard days, and every days.

–*Dan and Becky Kimball,* author of several books,
pastor of Vintage Faith Church, and speaker

"When I think back to my childhood, one memory sticks out over all the noise; every morning I would walk down the stairs and find my mom sitting in her chair, Bible open, pen in hand, eyes focused but distant. She was *hearing* the one voice that could bypass her deafness. My mom taught me how to listen to God; this book will do the same for you."

–*John Mark Comer,* pastor for teaching and vision at
Bridgetown: A Jesus Church in Portland, Oregon
and author of *Loveology* and *Garden City*

"*He Speaks in the Silence* is a beautiful read. Diane's unashamed vulnerability instantly draws you in and find yourself lost in her story—one where she freely admits her own insecurities and struggles with trust, faith, and understanding. Her honesty encourages you to seek and value silence, to make space to comprehend your own journey deeper, and to truly press into the One who speaks in that silence. It's about seeing beauty where there seems to be none, about believing through doubt, about pursuing a wild hope. I highly recommend this book!"

–*Sarah A. Dubbeldam,* Co-Founder, Editor-in-Chief
and Creative Director, *Darling Magazine*

"Diane Comer's personal journey from disappointed good girl to deeply spiritual woman of God shows the power of the Spirit's working in the midst of tragic loss when the eyes of faith opened deaf ears to hear the gently powerful voice of the LORD Most High. It will take you deep into intimacy with Him."

–*Gerry Breshears,* Ph.D., Professor of Theology,
Western Seminary, Portland, Oregon

HE SPEAKS IN THE SILENCE

FINDING
INTIMACY WITH
GOD
BY LEARNING
TO LISTEN

DIANE COMER

ZONDERVAN

He Speaks in the Silence
Copyright © 2015 by Diane Comer

This title is also available as a Zondervan ebook.
Visit www.zondervan.com/ebooks.

Requests for information should be addressed to:
Zondervan, 3900 Sparks Dr. SE, Grand Rapids, Michigan 49546

Library of Congress Cataloging-in-Publication Data

Comer, Diane.
    He speaks in the silence: finding intimacy with God by learning to listen /
Diane Comer.
        pages cm
    Includes bibliographical references.
    ISBN 978-0-310-34179-6 (softcover)—ISBN 978-0-310-34178-9 (ebook)—ISBN
    978-0-310-07022-1 (mobile app) 1. Christian women—Religious life. 2. Spirituality—
    Christianity. 3. Spiritual life—Christianity. 4. Listening—Religious aspects—Christianity.
    5. Deafness—Religious aspects—Christianity. I. Title.
    BV4527.C6336 2016
    248.8'6—dc23   2015028432

Published in association with William K. Jensen Literary Agency, 119 Bampton Court, Eugene, Oregon 97404.

Art direction: Curt Diepenhorst
Interior design: Kait Lamphere

First printing November 2015 / Printed in the United States of America

For Phil.

You have loved me through it all.

And for

John Mark, Rebekah, Elizabeth, and Matthew.

This is the whole story.

Contents

Prologue

I live in a world of silence.

Surrounded by sound, I hear nothing.

Not a chirp or a chime or a rustle in the wind. No bells or rings or banging or blaring. When the doorbell rings and the dog barks, I cannot hear. When the smoke detector shrills in protest at the whiff of a scorched meal left too long to simmer, I putter heedlessly on.

A child's whisper is lost to me. When her dimpled fingers pull me near, eyes twinkling, to share that secret with me alone—it is muzzled by silence. How I wish she'd say it again . . . and again, until I get it right.

I ache to hear my husband, my lover, the one who shares that part that no one sees. Those tender words of intimacy, the wild bliss of ecstasy, of two becoming one and all those sounds of passion. I miss that. Long for it.

The lap of water on the shore, the crackle of a fire that beckons, the crunch of leaves underfoot.

I feel the emptiness of not hearing the tinkle of rain on the roof, or the thrum of the anxious hummingbird's hovering. I miss even that frightful bass of a spring storm booming thunderous power across the skies outside my window; such silent impotence brings a blandness even to nature's majesty.

The quiet of my world throbs with sounds I cannot hear—those sounds that no longer summon, warn, delight, or soothe me.

Because I am deaf.

Completely, irrevocably, incurably deaf.

This is my story of losing my hearing, of nearly losing my faith, of coming precariously close to losing all I hold dear in the process.

And it is the story of how God picked me up out of the pit I so heedlessly dug myself into, brushed away the filth of my faithlessness, and set my feet on solid rock.

On Jesus. Himself.

Mine is not a pretty story. I wish it were.

I wish I could tell you my faith held me strong in the storms of life. That all the years of discipline and doing right stood me in good stead when faced with difficulty. I wish you could be proud of the way I handled hardship, that you could follow my sterling example so that you, too, could soar when hard things happen.

But that would be a lie, and I've lived enough of those.

Mine is a story, instead, of my complete and utter failure . . . and of God's relentless faithfulness in spite of me. It is a story of pursuit, of God going after me, of seeing glimpses of beauty in the midst of ugliness, of wanting more, of longing. Of wishing for what I did not have.

Mine is a story of learning to listen in the silence. Of figuring out how God speaks and why I miss so much and how to hear Him better, clearer, nearer.

I write this story and open up all the ugliness of my hidden self with the wildest hope that the One who rescued me, the One whose voice I have learned to cherish, will speak to you. And I pray as I write that you will listen.

For I have learned that *He speaks in the silence.*

From my heart,
Diane

CHAPTER 1

In the Beginning . . .

a story I didn't want

At first it was the little things.

I remember standing outside one warm afternoon, saying good-bye to my friends with their babies and toddlers. We'd spent the morning talking, as women do, about our hopes for our children and what their futures might hold. All the way out to their minivans, we were chatting away animatedly while our children ran in circles, loth to go home to quiet and naps.

Suddenly all my friends were silent, looking at me with question marks where their eyebrows rose.

"What? What's the matter?" I hurriedly inventoried my kids. Had something happened?

"Aren't you going to get that?"

Still confused, I just stared back at my friends, at all those worried eyes.

"The phone! Aren't you going to get the phone?" The incredulous look on their faces brought me up short.

These were the days before cell phones or texting or email or even answering machines. To not answer that phone hanging on the kitchen wall was rude, even risky. It could be important. It might be an emergency. No one ignored that insistent bell tone. Ever.

Suddenly, in the shocked silence of my friends, I heard the barest whisper of a ring. Again. "Oh my!" I dashed off to get it, heart thumping, breathless—not from the run across my suburban lawn, but from the terrible realization that what I'd been hiding could no longer be ignored.

Ever since a bout with pneumonia a few months before, I'd been having trouble hearing. Nothing drastic, just some subtle hints that perhaps my ears were plugged. Yes, I'd missed hearing the phone ring a few times, gotten impatient with everyone's mumbling, failed to wake up when my alarm buzzed. But with all the delightful chaos of my busy household, who could blame me? Babies and toddlers and sleep deprivation could easily explain my fumbles, couldn't they? Surely I was making a big deal out of nothing. The eyebrows covertly raised behind my back by my husband only irked me more, and I lashed out at him in annoyance, a thin veil over my fear.

That ringing phone would become my nemesis, underscoring what I was trying to deny. When I did happen to hear it ring, I couldn't tell who was on the line. All voices began blending into sameness. I couldn't tell the difference between Lynn and Kim and the gym. Once, I carried on a confusing conversation for ten minutes with Stacey, only to discover I was talking to Lucy.

Alarm clocks were becoming useless. Cookies burned in the oven while the buzzer droned silently. The frogs along the creek bed lost their voices. Birds failed to sing. What was happening?

One worn-out Monday morning, I gathered my rambunctious little ones, swaddled the baby, and drove the few miles to my parents' house. There on the back porch, in that familiar place where I'd once talked to her about boys and love and breakups and all the angst of teenage life, I poured out my fears to my mom. Over coffee and thick toast smeared lavishly with her homemade jam, the tears overflowed.

Before now, I'd told her nothing of my worries, pretending that everything was fine. In our family, when I was growing up, complaining was met most often with a stern rebuke. My parents' zero tolerance policy on whining kept us careful to edit our troubles and temper our grievances. Mom's practical, can-do attitude just didn't sit well on the shoulders of negativity. But that day, she listened with all the compassion of a mother who hears and knows. She entered into my angst, holding out her arms to embrace me when the sobs came bursting from where I'd tucked them deep inside.

"You have to *do* something," she insisted. "Get this checked out, and the sooner the better."

My ever sensible mother couldn't fathom her twenty-six-year-old daughter's reluctance to admit she was having trouble hearing.

"Why in the world haven't you made an appointment with a hearing specialist?" She set down her coffee, as if to get up and do it herself. "Make that phone call by the end of the day, or I will!"

A few months earlier, I'd taken my son to a specialist to have his ears checked after a series of ear infections. With my mother's words propelling me to action, I now made another call to the ear doctor, this time for myself. The receptionist spoke with the over-enunciated diction hearing professionals use on every patient, yet I shuddered at her assumption that I was calling because I was *one of those.*

I made an appointment for the following week and immediately regretted it. *I was fine.* I could hear. Did I really need a babysitter for my infant and two toddlers for half a day while I drove across town through traffic, just so they could tell me I was tired and needed to listen better?

But between my mother's pushing and my husband's insinuating—those eyebrows that repeatedly told me I'd missed yet another verbal clue—I knew it was time to capitulate. I'd go. Hopefully the doctor would give me a pill, and I'd hurry home to life as it was supposed to be.

The low-slung building with its outdoor corridors shadowed by deep redwood eaves was typical of California medical offices. A fountain trickled cheerily, raining drops of mist on my arm as I searched for the suite that housed the offices of nearly a dozen ear, nose, and throat specialists. Finding the carved door with Otology Services on a plaque above it, I hesitated. Could this be it? Otology was a term foreign to me, and it sounded enough like oncology to make me leery. But spotting the specialist's name carved into a brass plaque, I pushed open the door with a shudder of dread.

In the Beginning . . .

A bell tinkled as I entered, one more confirmation that I was most certainly wasting my time by coming here. See, I could hear! When the receptionist handed me a half dozen pages of questions to answer, I sat down with a sigh. Like it or not, I was here, waiting for what I was certain would be a simple prescription to clear up the muffled sensation in my ears.

The bland beige of the waiting room complemented the stoic expressions on the faces of the people waiting silently for their turns. Tan industrial carpeting, grass cloth-covered walls, seats stained by too many people sitting too long to hear what they couldn't hear. My insides churned.

Every other person in the waiting room looked old to me. A noiseless cloud seemed to hang over everyone who came through the door. A man with a cane hobbled in, sat down with a sigh, and shouted at his poor wife, who was trying to fill out forms. From across the room, I sensed her frustration and was embarrassed for both of them. Huge flesh-toned hearing aids hung on his ears, doing little to alleviate his confusion. My grandpa had worn those hideous things.

When my name was called, I couldn't seem to help rambling apologetically to the nurse. "Nothing's wrong, just a little muffling. I need to get this cleared up, just fluid in my ears, I'm sure." She nodded and led me to a sterile exam room to wait for the doctor.

For what seemed like forever, I waited in the silence of that room, so unlike the pediatricians' offices where a mama of three little ones spends so much time. Here there were no outcries, no laughter ringing. I swung my foot and tapped my fingers impatiently, wishing I hadn't come.

The doctor knocked once and entered, then shook my hand without looking at my face and stood with his back to me while mumbling something about a busy day. I immediately disliked him.

My first impression was that he was all one color. His blondish hair was fading into the same dull gray as his eyes and skin. Everything about him was precise. Every hair combed carefully in place, fingernails trimmed square, lab coat pressed to perfection. I tensed in his presence, feeling messy and mistaken, the haphazardness of my young-mother uniform of yoga pants and Reeboks highlighting my imperfections.

Staring at a folder in his lap, he asked a few questions.

"Your father has some hearing loss?"

"Yes, but just a little. His isn't too bad, really."

What did this have to do with my father? I was half his age, for heaven's sake.

"I wrote there that it started in the army while he was doing weapons testing. Too much exposure to loud noise, that's what his doctors said."

He let my comment thud like a rock in the middle of the room, never lifting his head from my file. Not so much as a nod or a hint that he had heard me. His fingers drummed the desk noiselessly.

I felt like I needed to defend myself from this cold man's insinuations. As if it was my fault I had a father with trouble hearing. As if maybe my own recent struggles might somehow be related.

"And your grandfather? He wore hearing aids."

"He was old. In his eighties. And then he only wore them when he felt like it. He never did think he needed them."

"Mmh."

This man's wordless expression made me want to prove him wrong. I was *not* hard of hearing. I was young, in the thick of raising a family. I wasn't "disabled," for Pete's sake!

He pulled out a set of brushed metal instruments with handles and prongs, like strangely elongated forks. He proceeded to tap each one on the table, asking if I could hear the sound. He was impatient when I didn't respond quickly. The dull tap on the table was clear enough, but what sort of sound was this strange instrument supposed to make?

Tap, tap, tap . . . then nothing.

He wouldn't look at me. Just tapped and frowned and wrote in his file. He moved the fork-shaped metal closer to my ear. Ah, there was something! I could feel the faintest vibration. Now everything would be okay.

I stared at him, willing him to look me in the face, wishing he would speak, wanting to fill the silence in that stark room, needing to see some hint of reassurance in his dull gray eyes.

Nothing.

Finally, he stood up, closed his file, carefully slipped the metal instruments into their felt-lined case, mumbled something I missed, and left the room. I stared at the door, subdued by his rudeness.

My ordeal wasn't over.

The nurse came back and led me through a labyrinth of offices, past closed doors and through the waiting area into the strangest room I'd ever seen. Pulling open the thick steel door guarding the entrance, she escorted me into a soundproof booth the size of a closet and gestured for me to sit in the chair in the center. The room reminded me of the nuclear bunkers I'd seen advertised in magazines while I was growing up in the midst of the Cold War era. The carpet muffled all sound, and the walls and ceiling were covered in perforated metal the color of putty. Stark, bland nothingness. On the floor were scattered a few children's toys, which she picked up with some grumbling.

I had no idea what was going on since no one seemed in the least inclined to communicate.

Then another lab coat shrouded professional walked in, this one with her hand extended. Like a fresh breeze in that stale tomb, Dr. Janna Smith-Lange shook my hand, smiled, and started to explain the process she was there to take me through. While she talked, I stared at her in wonder. Bright blond hair cut in a blunt bob, red lipstick, sparkling blue eyes—she exuded glamour. I sensed her warm caring as she looked me in the eye and squeezed my hand, as if to say, "We're going to be friends, you and I."

Later I learned that Dr. Smith-Lange, who eventually became simply "Janna" to me, had a PhD in audiology and spent her days testing all levels of hearing. Her clients were, for the most part, older people with years of decline already behind them and a few bouncing-off-the-walls toddlers with fluid-filled ears. Every once in a while, someone like me walked into her sound booth. Someone who shouldn't be there.

For the next hour, I listened for beeps and dings with long, silent stretches in between. I was instructed to click a handheld button whenever I heard a sound. Any sound. And there I sat, knowing I was missing tones, holding still, then leaning forward, trying harder to hear what I knew must be there. I'd hear something and click the button as fast as I could. More silence. Then a series of beeps I could actually hear. I pounded the button triumphantly! Then more silence. Long silence.

Deafening silence.

We proceeded to sentences. *The cowboy went into town. The airplane flew overhead. And single words like toothpaste, sidewalk, ice cream.* Janna had me repeat words while she covered her mouth with her manicured hand and made check marks in her file. I really didn't like that part. I knew I was guessing, confused by words that sounded the same, missing too many. I began to get the distinct impression that something was terribly wrong, that no one was going to just give me a pill and send me home.

My chest tightened with growing dread.

When we were finally finished, it seemed to take all of Janna's professionalism to keep herself from wrapping her arms around me and holding me close. Her compassionate gaze nearly undid me. I blinked back the tears gathering in my eyes. With tender care, she led me into the doctor's book-lined office and left me there.

Alone.

I'd never sat in a physician's personal office before. Until that day, my encounters with doctors were always in exam rooms. The nurse ushers you in, bids you to sit on the too-high table and wait. After a while, the doctor comes in and asks questions, sometimes pausing to poke and prod to see what the trouble is. Fluorescent lights hide nothing, and that's the point. The patient is there to be fixed, seeking a solution to whatever it is that troubles her.

But this room was dark, richly decorated with mahogany furniture, hunter green walls, and crackled leather chairs. I itched to open the blinds. My heart beat too hard.

After I waited for what seemed like an interminable time, the gray doctor walked in and sat behind his desk, placing my file precisely in the middle, and glanced at me. His eyes registered nothing. I don't think he saw me at all. He didn't see the young mother I was. He didn't know I had a family and a husband and babies—people I needed to hear. He didn't care about my hopes and dreams for the future. He looked right through me. I was just another patient with a file full of loss.

I sat trembling before him. By now I could sense the gravity of my diagnosis. I braced myself for what he had to say, pulling myself in tight lest I lose my tentative grip on control.

"Young lady, you have a severe hearing loss. It's caused by nerve damage, I'm certain. There is no excess fluid, no infection. Your pattern is typical of this kind of loss. I'm not sure what caused it, but it is almost certainly progressive . . . would expect deafness . . . hearing aids might help . . ."

Wait!

He lost me there. *Hearing aids? Me? What is he saying? I can hear! I'm twenty-six years old. I don't need hearing aids. He doesn't know what he's talking about. Hearing aids are for old men and handicapped people, not for me.* I choked back the tears threatening to erupt into a howl of denial.

"Can't you give me something for this? It's got to be connected with when I had pneumonia a few months ago." My interruption only seemed to intensify his coldness.

Pointing to my chart, he tapped the file to the staccato beat of his words, "I said no. No infection, no fluid. Your ears look normal."

"How can I have—what did you call it—'a significant hearing loss'? and my ears look normal? Something's not normal here!" I think my insistence shocked him out of his blandly clinical report just enough for him to really look at me.

"We'll do tests, of course. But because the loss is significant and similar in both ears, I suspect a genetic cause. Still, I'll order an MRI just in case."

I didn't dare ask, *in case of what?* I could tell he wanted me out of his office as much as I wanted to leave. My mind was too packed with protests to think clearly, so I plastered a polite smile on my face and thanked him for his time. Shaking, I nearly stumbled on my way out the door of his oppressive office, making my way to the receptionist to schedule a plethora of tests in the weeks ahead. As she loaded me up with a thick stack of papers, the pit in my stomach started to swallow me. Filled with a near-panicked need to flee, I fumbled to close the door behind me, acutely aware of the sounds I should be hearing but wasn't. The metallic clink of the latch was distinctly absent.

Outside, the clear blue California sky seemed to mock me. How could the sun shine cheerfully on such a day as this? How dare the people bustling past me smile and laugh? How cruel a joke that life just went on when I felt mine stop with the doctor's conclusive words.

Severe hearing loss . . . progressive.

I walked to my car, parked on the curb of the busy street, attuned to every sound. *Where was the click of my heels on the pavement? Shouldn't my keys jingle? Why did the rush of cars going by sound so far away?*

But it was when I glanced into the car that my heart froze. Crammed into the back were three car seats, one for each of my most treasured hopes. Empty now, those vacant seats represented my purpose, my delight, my calling. My family was my world.

Suddenly, I knew what drowning feels like.

A sinking, clawing, panicked choking out of life enveloped me.

I'm not sure how I managed to drive home that day. My eyes were dry, but my head hammered with questions. My soul felt on fire, a raging inferno of what-ifs.

What if it's true? What if I lose all my hearing? What if the doctors can't stop the loss? What about my baby? Can I care for her without sound? What if my toddlers can't talk to me? What if my someday-teenagers turn away from a mama who can't listen? Would my husband turn his back on me?

Phil's life was music. As the worship pastor of our church, his livelihood and focus was all wrapped up in sound. *How could I help him if I couldn't hear? Would he still love me? How would we communicate?*

On and on, the questions drove me home. When I pulled into the driveway of our ranch-style house in San Jose, my son burst out the front door, jabbering as he ran to greet me. Playing with his dad that morning had filled him with the little-boy delight I loved. His little sister tumbled out behind him, looking disheveled and confused. *Where have you been,* her upturned face seemed to ask.

Phil knew immediately that something was wrong. I'd been gone for hours, and now I held myself at a rigid distance. The concern in his eyes threatened to undermine my resolve to be strong.

"What's wrong, Di? What'd he say?" He handed me our squirming newborn, giving me just the distraction I needed to hold my terror in check. Saying as little as possible, I busied myself with the baby, letting him know he could go back to work now. I could do this—I would handle it. I must be strong.

I don't know how I managed to hold myself together enough to pretend I was fine in front of my children. I guess it's just a secret strength mothers have, or the result of years and years of craving control. I stuffed everything inside, kept myself reined in tightly, and willed the diagnosis to be wrong.

By the time the sun set that day, I had determined I would not be a drama queen, would not give in to hysterics. Phil had been plying me with questions ever since dinner, at a loss as to why I wouldn't answer. With the children tucked into bed, we found our favorite spot on the back porch, the quiet of the night wrapping us in a cocoon of calm as I related the sequence of events that led to the doctor's diagnosis.

"He thinks this hearing loss is permanent. He called it 'nerve damage.' He said both ears are perfectly fine but the signal they gather is getting short-circuited by some sort of damage to the cochlear nerve. It's the way most old people lose their hearing."

Phil couldn't help but interrupt me there, leaning forward as if to challenge me, "Old people? How can that be? If anyone should lose their hearing young, it'd be me. All those years of playing drums in the band—you didn't even like rock music!"

"I told him that too. It didn't seem to faze him at all. Mostly he talked about my dad and grandpa being hard of hearing. He wants more tests to find the cause, but it's clear on my chart, Phil. Something is causing my hearing to be really bad, worse than I'd thought."

"But isn't there some medicine you can take? Surely there's something this doctor can do." I could see Phil trying to fix this, wanting to rescue me.

Instead of answering, I told him about the audiologist—her bright hair and brighter lipstick, her ebullient way of letting me know she cared. He laughed as I regaled him with a description of the testing room that reminded me of a Cold War-era bomb shelter.

What I couldn't do was tell him the whole story. The doctor had been clear that he believed my hearing loss would follow a progressive, downward path toward deafness. But I couldn't say that now; I couldn't speak words I didn't want to believe. I knew that once I said the words, they'd have to be true. A little bit of hearing loss I could learn to live with. Deafness was something else entirely.

If indeed my auditory nerves were disintegrating, if my future looked anything like the doctor thought it would, then nothing would ever be the same.

But God could fix this. He could heal me.

It wasn't until the deep hours of the night when my baby woke for a feeding that the terror that He might *not* came crashing in on me. As I took my newborn in my arms, tears heaved up like a volcanic eruption.

I have a baby and I'm going to be deaf. Deaf! God, how could this be? How do You expect me to raise children who love You when I can't even hear them?

Tears flowed down my face, dripping off my chin. I couldn't wipe them away fast enough, couldn't stop sobbing, couldn't quell the panic rising within me.

I can't lose my hearing! I can't do this. I don't want to be deaf! Please, God!

When my cries woke Phil from a deep sleep, he tried fruitlessly to comfort me. "It's okay, Di, it's going to be all right. We'll figure this out. I'll call another doctor. Shh, shh, you'll wake the kids."

Nothing he said helped. It *wouldn't* be, couldn't be all right. I rocked back and forth with my baby in my lap, sobbing out my fear of what lay ahead, inconsolable, terrified.

All that night, I paced and cried and rocked as wave after wave of panic rolled over me. I stared into a future without sound, and the imagining left me in horror and despair.

That night was the beginning of a journey I wasn't ready for. One that would change me forever.

CHAPTER 2

A Keeper of Rules . . .

a story that wasn't real

In the days and weeks following the doctor's diagnosis, I was nearly overwhelmed with anxiety. I tried and tried to stuff it down inside, but the beast kept clawing its way back to the surface, chasing peace far away.

In the quiet of the night, my heart ached with the worry of wondering. I'd dreamed of sitting on the edge of my daughters' beds, listening, laughing, loving them as they grew into women. I'd imagined my son, John Mark, calling home someday from far away to boast to his mom of challenges faced and won. How would I know my children if I couldn't hear them?

What would become of my friendships? Unlike men, who manage to find satisfaction while fishing side by side without exchanging a word, women talk. We laugh at each other's missteps and cry over each other's heartaches. Women are bound together by words—lots and lots of words. We spend hours on the phone, talking through the intricacies of relationships and decisions. Surely my friends would abandon the effort of trying to talk to a woman who could not hear.

I dreaded being relegated to the silent backroom of the deaf. Every time I missed what someone was saying, every time I asked, "What? What was that? I don't understand you," the horizon of my future darkened still more.

Every day I lost a little more of my hearing. Every day wrenched me a little farther away from my children's boisterous voices, from my husband's intimate whispers. I had no time to garner control and figure it out. Deafness would not wait for me to catch up.

None of my familiar methods of coping were enough to protect me from my bitter reality.

Always before, I'd let bad news fly through one ear and out the other, never giving it a chance to land. For me, that mostly meant not talking about it, changing the subject when people asked, adopting a strategy of *If I don't think about it, it will go away.*

My dreams of a life filled with thriving relationships were disintegrating. The strategies and coping mechanisms that had worked for the minor bumps and bruises of everyday living weren't working now. I wasn't sure how I would survive this.

Somehow I'd managed to dodge, duck, or deny any significant pain in my life until then. At twenty-six, I'd never lost anyone close to me. I'd never tasted soul-killing rejection. My parents had been diligent guardians of life as it ought to be, and my husband had swept me off my feet and carried me over any minor bumps in the road that might stub my polished toes. I'd handled the hard things such as hurt feelings or pressure or not getting what I wanted with a neat formula: I'd just give myself a good talking to, plaster a smile on my face, and carry on.

Everything under control.

Simple. Doable. Nice.

Now, I was sinking, and I didn't know who or what to hold onto. The perfect pastor's wife, perfect mother, perfectly-in-control-got-it-together paradigm of the perfect woman just couldn't play perfect anymore.

But I was ill-prepared for anything else.

I was raised in a world of rules and roles and manners, of right and wrong. Women wore dresses and gloves and pretty hats stuck to their hair with pearl-tipped pins. Men took their hats off indoors, gave their seats to ladies, and carried carefully pressed handkerchiefs in their back pockets.

I have always liked the rules.

Rules make life safe, predictable. When I know the rules, I know how to act, what to do, and what to avoid at all costs. Rules have been the outline of my days, the parameters within which I have had the freedom to color and create.

As long as I stayed inside the lines, I felt safe. Acceptable. Right.

My family followed the rules. My mom relished her role as a mother—baking cookies, keeping our home clean and organized and running smoothly, creating and reading stories, sewing my clothes. Once a week, she donned her Boy Scout den mother uniform—navy blue skirt, tucked-in blouse, yellow scarf around her neck. I thought all moms were like that.

Dad was a hardworking man. Born into poverty, he'd pulled himself out of that pit with unwavering willpower. He worked his way through college, graduating debt free and determined to provide a better life for his family. We were the center of his universe, the reason to knot his tie every morning, pick up his briefcase, slip on his wingtips, and go to work. Every day, Dad left the house at the same time, and every day, he came home— like clockwork. We sat down to dinner together at night, talking about school and learning and the latest edition of the *National Geographic* magazine that sat on our coffee table.

And we went to church. Every Sunday, we put on our best clothes, shined our shoes, climbed into our Rambler station wagon, and drove to church. There, we dutifully listened to a dull message about God blessing us when we're nice and good and follow the rules. The organ played, a choir sang, we recited creeds about the Father, the Son, and the Holy Ghost (which always gave me the willies since my mother insisted there were no such thing as ghosts). We'd file out after the benediction to shake the hand of the Reverend in his dark robe and silk stole. The stole and the altar cloth were made of the same material and always matched. It was one of the rules: scarlet at Christmastime, white at Easter.

Very pretty and very right.

When I was ten, my family packed up everything in our nice suburban home in California and moved to Germany. An opportunity had come up for my dad to advance in his career and expand the possibilities for our family. On weekends, the five of us piled into our Opel sedan and toured Europe together. Dad drove while Mom directed traffic, two backwoods farm kids relishing a world they'd hardly known existed. Reading from her stash of green Baedeker guidebooks, Mom insisted that we learn and discover our way through enchanted lands. When we got to squabbling in the backseat, Dad and Mom would pull over and set up a picnic on the side of the road. Salami and cheeses and bakery bread washed down with fresh apple cider. I thought every family ate mom-made cookies while overlooking the Alps, the Riviera, or yet another castle.

In Germany, I attended a small, prestigious private school. My friends were from nations all around the globe. Their fathers were diplomats and bankers and international businessmen. The popular kids spoke several languages and traveled to exotic locations like Portugal and Tanzania for vacation. They were headed to Oxford or Yale or the Hebrew University of Jerusalem. Every student was required to be fluent in English and German and was strongly urged to master French as well. Our "elective" class choices were two: French, taught by a flamboyant Frenchman with a disdain for English, or Study Hall, guarded by Miss Moroni, our much maligned math teacher.

In that environment, rules reigned. No skipping in the halls, no derogatory names, no short skirts or straggly hair. We got black checks in the Teacher's Book if we slipped up and spoke English in French class, red checks if we got an answer right. It was a world of headmasters and fancy lab equipment and diplomacy and doing well. Behaving. Being good.

I felt safe in that world.

I was instructed in how to be a good girl, and I rose to the challenge with no great effort or angst.

I was fourteen when my dad was transferred back to the States. When I started high school, I discovered that the place I'd left wasn't the same as the one I came back to. The rules had changed, and I didn't know what they were.

I knew next to nothing about the latest fashions (the J.C. Penney catalog had been our trusty style guide while living overseas) or the right bands or the hip way to talk. In the early 1970s, cool was out and bummer was in. Guys were foxes and pretty girls were chicks. The new Farah Fawcett hairstyles required blow dryers and curling irons in order to feather our bangs just right.

I was neither cool nor foxy, and my mass of stick-straight hair refused to feather.

I didn't fit—anywhere.

In a mad scramble to belong, I started messing up my life, creating knots that could have taken a lifetime to untie, like the time I snuck into the liquor cabinet in the dining room and poured just a little bit of about a dozen different bottles into an empty peanut butter jar. I sloshed that jar to school and hid it in my locker. Kids lined up for a taste of that nasty concoction, and for one full day I had friends.

In the seventies, American kids smoked cigarettes in the parking lot at school; they rolled weed and went to parties with beer kegs purchased for them by their country club parents. They swore and made out in the school hallways and booked rooms in the San Francisco Fairmont Hotel after the prom. Kids at school persuaded me to sneak out of my room after my parents went to bed, to party on the beach in Santa Cruz. The sure way to acceptance was to be daring and bad.

To break the rules.

That's when the church stepped in to rescue me.

We'd been looking for a church to attend since we'd gotten back from Germany. Most good suburban Americans still went to church in the early 1970s. Christmas and Easter were a must, but many families even went in between holidays. In Germany, my parents had been given a Living Bible during one of our frequent visits to an army base near our home. Though we were not military, our passports allowed us on the base to go to church or to dine on familiar American food at the officers' club. The chaplain's warmth and easy ways encouraged my parents to learn more than the little they'd known before. Intrigued, they set out to find a different kind of church when we got home, though we had no clue what criteria to apply.

More than anything else, I had a compelling ache to belong that pushed me to search, to meet a longing deep inside for more.

One church was too "out there," another too liturgical, another seemed unfriendly. Then one Sunday, we drove by a traffic jam on the way to Los Gatos, my mom's favorite place to hunt for antique furniture. Cars were lined up, snaking slowly into the parking lot of a converted electronics warehouse. Police officers were directing traffic. When we saw from the sign that the building was a church, we knew we had to try it.

The very next week we did, and we were immediately captivated. The preacher addressed the congregation in a normal business suit, the kind my dad wore to work every day. He talked in a perfectly ordinary tone of voice using everyday words as he taught out of a big black Bible. What he said made sense. Everyone seemed friendly and full of life, as if they enjoyed church and liked each other and knew something I didn't.

I begged my mother to bring me back. "This is it. This is the church we need to go to, this is what we've been looking for!"

The very next week and every week thereafter, all five of us filed into a row of metal folding chairs to hear a message of hope, to learn about a God who wanted a relationship with each of us. Somehow we had missed that in all our years of churchgoing.

Mom, with her guileless, extroverted ways, made friends right away. One of those friends coerced her daughter, who went to my school, to invite me to youth group. I had no idea what a youth group was, but at my mom's insistence, I gathered up what little social courage I had and entered a whole new world. A band with bearded guitar players jammed on the stage, kids talked and laughed and hugged each other. Everyone carried paperback Bibles with *The Way* splashed across the cover.

Though I hardly understood what I was signing up for, I did know this: I'd have done just about anything to be a part of this group of people. I wanted what they had. I wanted them.

For several months, I sat in that church, surrounded by a sense of something more. I felt filled up there, as if just being in that place connected me with a God I hadn't sensed in all the grand cathedrals in Europe.

The youth group kids embraced me and swept me into their circle, where I met loving, fun, inclusive people who remembered my name. My new friends saved me a seat, gave me rides to Farrell's Ice Cream Parlor after the Sunday night service, told me they would pray for me, and made me feel like I belonged. Like I mattered. Like they liked me.

Slowly, the pieces were coming together.

At the end of his sermons, the preacher (no one called him Reverend) always invited people to "come forward" to "receive Christ" in the prayer room. There was no way I was going to do that! Raising my hand and walking to the prayer room in front of all those people would be mortifying. Besides, wasn't I already a Christian? I wasn't Muslim or Buddhist or atheist—after all, I was an American. Weren't we automatically Christian?

Nevertheless, I was intrigued, leaning in every week to listen and soak up everything I heard. I couldn't shake the feeling that I needed to do something, to make some sort of statement that I was "in." Six months later, a guest preacher gave what I'd learned was called "the invitation," and I felt compelled to respond. With my legs trembling so badly they could barely hold me up, I squeezed my way past packed-in knees in the row of metal chairs, avoiding feet and Bibles and purses, and "came forward."

I slipped into a corner of the prayer room as it filled up with many other people making a "decision for Christ." I repeated a prayer, just like the counselor told me to, and walked out of that room with a booklet, a pat on the back, and assurances that I was now "saved."

I'm still not sure if I really knew what I was doing. Nothing magical happened, no fireworks or grand revelations. I don't remember repenting of sins or even realizing I was a sinner. And yet, little by little, words about "redemption" and being "born again" had begun to penetrate. The message of the cross sank deep, a welcome relief to my striving for acceptance. I still thought I was a good girl who'd followed the rules, including the one that compelled me to reach out that day for salvation. But that step started me on a journey to know more, to know this One I now called my Savior. To be one of His followers. To follow His rules.

And so I set out to learn.

I'd signed up to follow Christ after hearing the emphatic promise that "God loves you and has a wonderful plan for your life." I liked that. A lot. A wonderful plan, a wonderful life. All I had to do was be good, do what was right, avoid the bad stuff. Then, God would make sure everything else fell neatly into line. Amen.

For most of my life, fear had dogged me. Fear of messing up socially had kept me shy and reserved, afraid to reveal too much of myself lest people reject me. Fear of hurting myself prevented me from conquering the ski slopes or pushing myself harder.

Fear of failure kept me from trying things, risking, daring, doing the unconventional.

I'd taken all that fear with me into my new faith, only now I called it caution. I would be careful. I would watch myself closely lest I "fall away." I would do everything required of me; I would follow the rules. Strict adherence, I was sure, would keep me safe now that I had given my life to God. I memorized those verses that seemed to promise His protection, reciting them whenever fear of any kind threatened my secure new world.

Every week, the preacher opened his Bible and taught about life in the kingdom, how it was different and how we were different and how Jesus was the One who made all the difference. Because everyone else did, I took notes, filling in my blanks of ignorance with this new knowledge. Simple truths that everyone else seemed to know made a profound impression on me. How had I missed this? I felt as if my world were being turned right side up.

For the first time, it all made sense.

I loved my new life as a Christian, and I worked hard to get it "right." To be disciplined. Committed. It didn't take long for my life to begin to change in earnest. I stopped swearing, though I had nightmares about the words popping out in front of my church friends. I threw away the cigarettes pilfered from a friend's mom and went to parties with the determined intent to "witness" to anyone who would listen.

Once the "major" sins were dealt with, I felt pretty good about myself, secure in my world. I was learning and growing and getting it right. I knew my friends loved me and so did my parents.

And why not? I was a good girl who followed the rules and did the right things and didn't mess up. No wonder God loved me. After all, He was getting a pretty good deal.

Surrounded by a sense of acceptance and security and the rightness of life, I inched out of my awkward shell and grew into the woman God intended me to be—or so I thought.

While I was learning and growing and shedding my shyness, an idea began to form in my mind about what the "right" man for me might look like. Sort of a combination of my absolutely solidly dependable dad, with the stature of evangelist Billy Graham and the charm of rock-and-roll drummer Ringo Starr. After reading the biography of missionary Jim Elliot, I threw him in there too.

And every week at choir practice, I silently swooned over the choir director, Phil Comer. He was way too old for me, of course, having graduated from college and now working on staff at the church as the worship leader. To him, I was just one of the dozens of silly girls who sang in his choir. For three years, I sat in the second row and studied him. When he quoted a book he'd been reading, I ran out and bought the book. When he pulled out 3x5 cards and urged us to memorize Scripture, I scurried to gather my own. Halfway through rehearsal, he'd often pull out his own Bible and teach us about relationships that honored God, total surrender to Christ, and living a sold-out life.

Phil's passion for God pulled me into a maelstrom of emotion. Who was this man? Would anyone like him ever notice me? Did I dare hope for a husband like him?

By the time I graduated from high school, I had an intense crush on Phil. When he casually asked me if I'd like to go hear a speaker at a Christian conference center one Friday night, I about came out of my skin. Phil Comer asking me out? Was it a date? Dare I hope?

That Friday, I made a mess of my till at the window of American Savings and Loan where I worked. I knew I wasn't good enough or godly enough or mature enough for this man. I was sure I'd be tongue-tied and ridiculous. I was so afraid to say the wrong thing that I was certain I wouldn't be able to speak at all.

When our first stop was at a hospital where a girl from the choir had been admitted that afternoon, I finally began to breathe as I observed his ease. Bringing me along into his world of pastoral care, he laughed and joked, then grabbed my hand as he prayed for the girl we were visiting. He urged me to pray with her as well, setting my heart to pounding as I fumbled through a quick prayer.

He was relaxed and confident, and he caught me up in his world by sharing his dreams for the future. We talked about what it might mean someday for him to do more than worship ministry at the church, about seminary and preaching and a life full of possibilities. By the time I got home that night, I would have agreed to elope right then and there. Here was a man I could trust—my ideal man. The right man for me. I was sure of it.

Our relationship, like everything else about Phil, was intentional and intense.

He swept me off my proverbial feet, painting a picture of a life of following God together, of living completely and entirely for

Him, of making a difference. I knew from the outset that life with Phil would stretch me beyond my nineteen-year-old self-centeredness. I knew I would spend many nights alone while he was off directing another choir or leading worship or practicing with the band. I knew we would never be rich, that we'd never retire to the mountains, that this man would spend his life serving Christ in whatever way he could.

I wanted it all! The life, the man, and the faith he inspired in me. On July 15, 1978, I promised to follow him wherever he led, to love him no matter what, in sickness and in health, for richer or for poorer, as long as we both shall live.

I would be a good girl extraordinaire: a perfect wife, an ideal woman.

What I hadn't yet learned was that good girls, over time, become self-righteous and bitter and brittle. You see, good girls don't do anything really wrong . . . and so they don't really repent . . . and even if they do (ten years ago I said something mean about my mama . . .), no one takes them seriously. They get no sympathy for sins that leave such seemingly superficial scars, whereas the woman who slept around and stole someone's husband and had an abortion and was addicted to something awful gets cheers and hugs and "you done good, girl!" from everyone in awe of the transformation. Good girls just get blank stares that don't veil the *You've got to be kidding me* thoughts lurking behind patronizing eyes.

And so good girls say nothing.

But something happens inside a good girl's soul over time. Something insidious and subtle.

The arteries between her head and her heart commence to clog. Sluggishness and complacency sets in. A sort of I've-heard-it-all-a-million-times kind of attitude begins to dull her appetite for spiritual truth, leaving her anemic and . . . bored.

That's where I found myself at the still tender age of twenty-six. I'd been married to a wonderful husband for seven years. We were partners in ministry. Phil was the ever up-front leader, while I relished leading discipleship groups and spent hours listening one-on-one, sharing other women's joys and heartaches.

Phil showered me with affection, giving me the life I'd always dreamed of. We'd moved from San Jose to be a part of a church plant in Santa Cruz, where our new home perched on a hill overlooking Monterey Bay. I spent my days doing exactly what I wanted to do: caring for our three young children and our cozy home. While we didn't have a lot of extras, we had enough.

But every moment of my days was filled with diapers and discipline and cleaning up messes and trying to get dinner on the table. And every day was exactly the same: wake up to a jangling alarm clock (if the baby didn't wake me first), dutifully check off my daily read-through-the-Bible-in-a-year plan, make breakfast for three famished kids, make beds, dress children, clean up the house, make lunch, put kids down for naps, clean up the house, keep kids from killing each other, stick kids in front of Sesame Street so I could make dinner, feel guilty about letting the kids watch Sesame Street, clean up the house . . . and fall exhausted into bed.

And these were supposed to be the most fulfilling years of my life!

At the time, feminism was redefining the role of women. Girls were expected to go to college and prepare for a career. We were being urged to crash through that infamous glass ceiling so many equated with bondage. In my own grandly defiant gesture of radical faith, I had quit college as soon as I got married. No selfish career track for me! Denying my inherent love of books and classrooms and all things connected to learning, I chose a different path. I would find fulfillment at home.

I read books about organization, color coordination, nutrition, time management, communication. I devoured everything ever written about ministry and hospitality and discipleship and child development. I signed up for a periodical that came in the mail every month, describing for this manic mama every sound that should be coming out of my baby's mouth and every milestone she certainly ought to have reached by today's date. No pacifiers for my baby—she was going to learn to converse intelligently and read fluently in record time. I was certain I could become the perfect wife and mom if only I tried hard enough.

And I loved my life—most of the time.

But sometimes, in the quiet of the night when I fell into bed exhausted with the housework unfinished, or in those early morning hours when I was first emerging into another day of more work, more messes, more meals, more dirty clothes, and sibling conflict, doubt nagged me. All I'd ever really wanted was to create a family with a man who loved me. This, I told myself, was what I was born for. I was fulfilling my calling, and surely I ought to be completely satisfied.

Yet something nagged uncomfortably down deep, making my days feel endless and my life seem like less than what I'd hoped for. Like a scratchy tag at the neck of my blouse, dissatisfaction irritated me just enough to keep the promise of my wonderful life a little itchy.

What was wrong with me? Shouldn't I be happier? I wasn't depressed, exactly, just a little disappointed. I thought living my dream would mean more. More happiness, more restfulness, and at least a little more of that elusive thing every woman wants: more satisfaction. Instead, I felt more and more empty.

For a long time I pushed aside these thoughts the moment they crowded to the surface. They felt disloyal, a betrayal of the love I relished for my family. I wanted to love my life. I needed to be happy with all these blessings. Maybe if I just tried harder, got up earlier, turned off Sesame Street, and read more books to my children, maybe then I'd feel it, this elusive thing I longed for.

I wasn't happy, not really. And I knew it.

For one full year, I'd been mentored by a woman by the name of Muriel Cook. Each week she'd spend an hour or more with me, opening my eyes to treasures she'd discovered in her daily reading of the Scriptures. Truths I'd mostly missed as I'd checked off my dutiful Bible reading chart. The lessons she shared with me made the stories come alive, the words applicable and rich. Each week I left in awe of the beauty that made her glow. I wanted to be like her. I wanted what she had.

One week she came into our session wiping tears from her cheeks. When I wondered why, she let me know that her tears were for her own frailties. She'd disappointed herself, done something or said something she knew wasn't right—sinned. I couldn't imagine what she was talking about. Muriel Cook sin?

Not possible. Her heartfelt confession made me take a long look at my own life. I'd never shed tears over sin. What was it that compelled Muriel into such honest intimacy with God?

And so I began to do the only thing I knew to do, the only thing a good Christian girl could do—I prayed. Every day, I asked God to do something, anything to change my heart. I prayed when I woke up, while jogging, while shopping, while cooking yet another family meal on yet another day of doing right.

I didn't pray once. Or even twice. I prayed every chance I got, as if by begging God, I'd get Him to hear me and He'd have to give me what I craved.

I needed more. I wanted more. I had to have more!

God knew I would need all of Him to face the days ahead. The journey that lay ahead of me was going to be more arduous than all my rule-abiding good-girl-ness would be able to handle. I would face dark days, days of discovering that I was not as good as I'd thought, that my façade wouldn't hold up under the pressures of life gone wrong, that a desperately "bad" girl lurked in my soul. That I was a woman who didn't know her true colors until she didn't get her way.

I was about to embark on a journey of facing the worst about myself and finding God in the rubble. In that place of desperation, I would discover that what God wanted more than all of my exhausting efforts to be good was me, just as I am.

The real me.

CHAPTER 3

The Fear and the Fury. . . .

a story fraught with danger

People said the strangest things when they heard about my failing hearing. The one I heard most often from well-meaning but misguided Christians was, *You're going to learn so much through this experience.* I wanted to scream every time someone said that to me. *Is that supposed to make it better?* I wanted to ask. *Really?*

I didn't feel like I was *learning,* all I felt was an enormous amount of frustration.

It is exasperating to want to talk to someone, to want to get to know them, but to be afraid to initiate a conversation I will likely not understand. Or to work so hard to wring out every intelligible bit of sound from the roar that meets my ears that I'm completely worn out from the effort.

It is frustrating to hear a well-meaning person say, "But you do so well, nobody would ever know!" What they don't realize is how much I miss, how often I bluff, how tense I get during a conversation when I hope I am nodding my head the right way. Or how stupid I feel when I see that look in their eyes that means I've just blundered badly.

The thought of being cut off, isolated and alone in my silent world, terrified me. And right on the heels of all that fear, anger followed.

Isn't that how it always works? Our child comes home late from the neighbor's house, and by the time he walks through the front door, we're ready to jump down his innocent throat.

Every time I came home from church worn out from the increasingly frustrating charade of pretending to hear, or I didn't hear the doorbell or couldn't understand my son, or I didn't hear the blaring sirens until the passing fire truck scared me witless, anger flared within me. Hot rage boiled just beneath the polished surface of my good-girl demeanor. As frightened as I was, my fear was eclipsed by the pulsing, festering, seething sense that God had wronged me. That all of this was, in fact, His fault.

When the "more" I ordered wasn't placed before me like a lobster dinner, I just tried harder to be good enough to win His blessing.

By the time I finished out my twenties, I was exhausted. I had earned a reputation for being a "good listener." I'm not sure all the reasons why, but women poured out their hearts to me. Part of it was because of my husband. Phil was a preacher and a worship leader, a spiritual giant kind of man. Everyone assumed that I would be too. Since I was kind of quiet, nodded my head a lot, and knew how to ask questions and sit still, women came to me to talk.

But after a while, instead of just listening, I began to offer advice. Good advice that sounded right and made sense to me. I got impatient, even angry, when they didn't follow it. After all, I would think, everyone knows right from wrong and you did wrong. Now go do right. Period.

Good girls don't know *how you could have* because *they never did* and are certain *they never would*, no matter what.

Deep inside, I was growing increasingly intolerant of other people's struggles.

A good girl knows enough not to act arrogant. She never boasts outright, never recounts her good-girl deeds. She's too good for that. Yet pride, subtle and softened by spiritual speak, slides past the sin sensors and creeps in like a cancer. And that cancer eats away at the spiritual nerve endings that make a person sensitive and responsive to the love of God.

A numbness sets in.

Sermons are for other people. *I wish so-and-so were here to hear that.* I found myself taking notes so I could preach to others, say it just right. I'd jot down verses so I would be ready to shoot them back in my next conversation with someone who was doing something wrong.

Good girls with good daddies tend to think God's love is a reward for their virtue. "If you love Me, you will keep My commandments"[1] becomes, "If you keep My commandments, you prove how much you love Me," and something gets lost in the translation. Spiritual life becomes more about me loving God, and not so much about the wonder of Him loving me.

49

Of course God loves me, just like my daddy does. I'm a good, loveable girl.

But God's love goes so much deeper than a father's love, and good girls just don't get it because they think they deserve all that loving. They don't feel guilty because they haven't really done anything wrong. Right?

My husband knew nothing of my self-righteous attitude. Before giving his life to Christ, he'd lived the rock band dream life. Abandoning the morals of his parents, he'd fully embraced reckless living, and in so doing, made a wreck of his life. When he'd been offered redemption, forgiveness, and a new start, Phil had abruptly turned his back on all that shame and flung himself full force into chasing after God. I could never let Phil know what was going on inside me now. He would never understand. Worse yet, he might see me as something less than he wanted me to be.

The truth was, I was becoming something less than I wanted to be—bitter that no one fully appreciated all my goodness, that no one was as impressed as it seemed they ought to be. And brittle because all that effort is exhausting. After a while, protecting that good-girl reputation wears a woman out. People start trying to shoot the good girl off her pedestal, and she begins to wobble when they do.

And woe to the world when a good girl falls.

Sarah was the epitome of a good girl.

She married Abraham at a respectably young age, followed him wherever he wanted to wander, set up housekeeping under the oak trees at Moreh, and made friends with her Canaanite neighbors. No complaining, no fuss. Adapting became Sarah's hallmark; she could be depended on to do the right thing. Always.

When famine forced the family to move again, Sarah cooperated. When Abraham felt threatened by the remote possibility that the ruler of Egypt (where he wanted to camp) might decide to kill him in order to have Sarah, she agreed to pretend to be his very available sister. Anything to save poor Abe's neck.

As it happened, Sarah's beauty was duly noted by the ever-vigilant paparazzi, who in turn told the king, who showered Abraham with gifts in exchange for Sarah. There she sat, surrounded by Pharaoh's harem girls, where she again made friends. A "terrible plague" broke out amongst Pharaoh's household, with drastic consequences. While everyone was searching heaven for a sign of why this was happening, word leaked out of the harem about a possible double cross. Pharaoh demanded to see Abraham, and when he did, he blistered the poor guy. "What is this you have done to me? Why didn't you tell me she was your wife? Why were you willing to let me marry her, saying she was your sister? Here is your wife! Take her out and be gone!"

At that point, Pharaoh sent his brawniest bouncers to escort the disgraced Abraham, his star-quality wife, and all their gear out of town. (Find the whole story in Genesis 12.)*

---

* I have taken creative liberties with Sarah's story, filling in the blanks with details that are not clear in Scripture. I do this with the intent of putting ourselves in Sarah's shoes, of seeing my own tendencies in her responses.

Years go by. Sarah is getting older. Every month her cycle starts, and every month she tells herself "next month." She sleeps with Abraham, and it stops being fun because all she can think about is having his baby. She tries again and again and again. Something must be wrong.

We can hear the typical good girl feel-sorry-for-me-bitterness creeping in: "The Lord has kept me from having any children."[2] So, Sarah being Sarah, she comes up with a viable, socially acceptable solution. "Why don't you have sex with my maid, Hagar?" (Hagar's name, coincidently, means "to come to or attack," which is exactly how the poor woman must have viewed Sarah's suggestion.) Abraham complies, and Hagar gets pregnant . . . and sassy. Sarah, with all the logic we women are renown for, turns on Abraham and tells him it's all his fault. "The Lord will make you pay for doing this to me!" she says.[3]

The now thoroughly shamed Abraham doesn't know what to do with his good-girl wife, so he does what every brow-beaten man does when he doesn't know what to do—nothing. "She is your servant, you may deal with her as you see fit," he says.

To which every woman reading this pulls out her hair and yells, "You wimp!"

Except Sarah. Now she's got permission, so good-girl Sarah gets mean. Really nasty, ugly, poke-you-where-it-hurts mean. And Hagar, probably still post-birth hormonal, takes off running into the desert.

End of story.

Actually, Sarah's story is just warming up. While Abraham's faith is increasing through encounter after encounter with God's emissaries, Sarah's faith is shriveling.

One day, when Abraham is sitting outside his tent, he looks up and sees three extraordinary men standing in front of him. He rushes to pay homage to what he is sure is a holy entourage, then dashes in to bark orders at Sarah. "Quick! Get three measures of your best flour and make some bread."

Can't you hear her banging pots in her makeshift kitchen? *Mutter, mutter, mutter. . . . Who does he think he is, always bossing me around? Doesn't he know it's hot in here? Has he no idea how long it takes to make bread? And three measures? Now he's giving me the recipe? Mutter, mutter, mutter . . .*

But, being the good girl that she is, Sarah rolls up her sleeves and starts to work.

She's also eavesdropping. Pausing to rub her aging back, she makes sure she doesn't miss a word of the conversation between these strange men and her husband.

"Where is Sarah, your wife?" one of them asks.

How do they know my name? Why are they asking about me? Sarah must be wondering. She moves closer to the tent flap.

"About this time next year I will return, and your wife Sarah will have a son."

Sarah barely manages to keep herself from laughing out loud! She's 89 years old at this point, well past the time to carry a child, and Abraham is ten years older.

Nothing much has been happening in their once hot bedroom for a very long time. A baby? From an old woman like me? Chuckling cynically under her breath, Sarah may not be talking out loud, but she's arguing skeptically on the inside. With a silent *hmpf!* Sarah goes back to her dough.

And here's where we see a typical good-girl deception. The Lord (turns out that's who's there) says to Abraham, "Why did Sarah laugh? Why did she say, 'Can an old woman like me have a baby?' Is anything too hard[4] for the Lord? About this time next year, I will return, and Sarah will have a son."

"Sarah was afraid, so she denied it. But the Lord said, "No, you did laugh."[5]

Sarah has been laboring under the guise of goodness for decades, but she still doesn't have the only thing she wants—a baby. I can imagine her thoughts. Oh, she's heard the promises. Again and again and again. It's all Abraham seems to talk about, and she's sick of it. *God* hasn't let her get pregnant,[6] it's Abraham's fault that things went south with her Hagar plan, and now see how easily she lies. To God, no less.

Sarah's story is so like mine, I shudder.

I wasn't barren and no Hagar shadowed my marriage and Phil never abandoned me to a harem. But all the themes are there: a good girl begins to blame God, turn bitter, and become intolerant of anyone who isn't as good as she is.

It didn't take much to convince me that God had done me wrong. After all, I had been trying to live a perfect life. I was loved, coddled, and protected, and I responded by trying hard to be good. My animosity at God's seeming indifference to my cries for help simmered to a steady boil. Ever since I'd become a Christian, I'd been so sure He would protect me. I'd swallowed every enticing word of the evangelical marketing scheme. But how was this "a wonderful plan for your life"? How was this evidence of Him being "in control"? I'd properly "cast all my cares on Him," and this was His response? Silence?

I spat embittered accusations against all I thought I'd known about God. Phrase by cross-stitchable phrase, I began dismantling everything I believed. After all my self-sacrificing, sin-denying striving to be righteous like He wanted me to be, all He'd done was nothing.

No help in time of need.

Every day, that nothingness flew in the face of my flailing faith. My hearing worsened. When the waitress at the restaurant asked me which dressing I wanted on my salad, I stared at her in perplexed confusion. I had no idea what that string of unintelligible words represented. And I took her impatient response personally—against God.

See? I'd mutter to the One who was supposed to take care of me. *This is what You're doing to me. Don't tell me that Your*

55

loving-kindness is new every morning, because if it was, I would have heard her!

Like an adolescent storming off to her room, I got the last word every time. Slamming the door in the face of God left me triumphant . . . and angrier still. He was weak, passive, uncaring, mean. And I had every right to let Him know I wasn't buying this God-is-love stuff.

And then I'd slip my perfect face back on, act like everything was fine, and ignore the churning in my gut.

In the parlance of hearing professionals, it's called "bluffing," and my audiologist refused to allow me to hone that skill. When, every few months, I sat down with her for yet another test, she'd be watching for my fakery, ready to pounce when I pretended to hear something I hadn't understood. And I was doing it with more than misunderstood sentences. I was bluffing my way through the awful realization that my hearing was failing much more rapidly than I or my doctors had expected, and my grip on the world of communication was going with it.

At church, I was raising my hands in worship while inside, I was shaking my fist at a God whose seeming indifference said to me that He didn't care.

A few months after my diagnosis, Phil accepted a job at a church in Santa Cruz. He went from being the worship pastor at a large church to a much broader position in a smaller church filled with new believers. Unlike the buttoned-up, conservative suburban church we had come from, most of these people were brand new to their faith. The innocence of our children brought hope to their brokenness and they embraced our family with purest love.

Oh, how those people worshiped! With hands held high, often barefoot, entirely oblivious about starched shirts and proper protocol, they sang and danced and delighted in their redemption.

I, on the other hand, grew more stiff and reserved. My response to my own brokenness was nothing like what I saw in these people. *I'm not like them,* the now-familiar self-righteous voice intimated. I had never done anything drastically bad. In contrast, their stories of disastrous marriages, drug use, and dirtiness repelled me. *They need to learn how to live right, to be good and clean and disciplined. Maybe I should show them how.*

To set a good example, on Sundays I always dressed my best. Hair curled and sprayed into place, hosiery and heels, matching handbag, just enough jewelry to pull it all together—I would show them what a Christian woman ought to look and act and be like. And yet my insides churned with a complicated mix of doing good and feeling bad.

The more I tried to pretend in public, the more all that volcanic, throbbing anger threatened to spew out of me onto innocent bystanders. And one day it finally did.

One weekend not long after we'd moved to Santa Cruz, I sat in the front row during worship, crying hot tears that refused to stay where they belonged, shaking my spiritual fist at God for His silent refusal to give me what I wanted. Fortunately for me, the worship ended before I melted down entirely.

As my husband took his place next to me, a man behind me tapped my shoulder.

"Uh, Diane, I need to tell you something," he said.

I turned to face him, shaking his extended hand as he pulled me in closer.

"I know about your hearing, Diane. I know what's happening."

I stiffened, trying to put a polite distance between myself and this strange little man. He was ugly, his face pocked, his neck sagging. He seemed barely able to hold himself erect.

"Diane," he insisted, refusing to let me back away, "God told me He is going to heal you!"

I froze.

Somewhere deep inside me, hope flared—and then died in the space of a heartbeat. *How dare he! Who did he think he was?* I turned on him faster than he could blink, spitting out bitter words.

"Well, He hasn't told me! Why would He tell you?" And with that, I swung around to face the front before more rage spewed.

My husband looked at me as if I'd lost my mind. I refused to return his glance, pulling away from his attempt to soothe my anger. Painfully aware that I'd broken my own code of perfect pastor's wife conduct, I sank deeper into my seat and hoped no one else had heard.

What was wrong with me? *What was wrong with God?* Why in the world would He tell this man that He was going to heal me? Why hadn't He told *me*? Why hadn't He answered my prayers? I had done everything He'd asked, obeyed every rule, made all sorts of sacrifices to stay in His good graces. *He owed me.*

It wasn't until much later that evening that Phil told me the man's story. Carefully, unsure of how I would react, he asked me about the brief, heated exchange. I cringed, ashamed of myself.

"Why would God tell him and not me? Why hasn't God healed me? Why? We've asked and asked and we hear nothing. My hearing just gets worse. I know I shouldn't have gotten mad, but really, Phil, what was he thinking?"

"Diane, John has cancer. That's why his face is all bent out of shape. His lymph nodes are swollen; those are scars on his neck. He asked the elders to pray for him last week after the doctors told him there is no hope. They're giving him less than six months to live."

Shame settled over my shoulders like a shroud. I'd sounded off to a dying man. After months of fighting and believing and trying, the verdict was in. John had lost. And instead of telling me his sorrows, he'd tried to lift mine. He'd been trying to instill in me the hope he held out for me. He believed right up until he died a month later that God would heal me.

Meanwhile, my frozen heart got a little harder every day.

God *could* heal me. Of course He could, He'd made my ears! With a snap of His fingers, He could save me from the silence. Supposedly, He'd told this dying man that He would.

All I knew was that He *hadn't* healed me. Nor had He healed John.

As C. S. Lewis watched his wife die, he wrote these words:

> Meanwhile, where is God? This is one of the most disquieting symptoms. When you are happy, so happy that you have no sense of needing Him, if you turn to Him then with praise, you will be welcomed with open arms. But go to Him when your need is desperate, when all other help is vain and what do you find? A door slammed in your face and a sound of bolting and double bolting on the inside. After that, silence. You may as well turn away.[7]

Like Lewis, I felt as though a door had slammed in my face with the sound of bolting and double bolting on God's side.

I was not alone in my sense that God was silent to my tantrums. Job heard the same nothingness. "I must express my anguish. My bitter soul must complain . . . I hate my life . . . I am disgusted with my life. Let me complain freely. My bitter soul must complain. I will say to God . . . why do you reject me . . . ?"[8]

And Naomi: "Don't call me Naomi," she responded. "Instead, call me Mara, [bitter] for the Almighty has made life very bitter for me. I went away full, but the LORD has brought me home empty. Why call me Naomi when the LORD has caused me to suffer and the Almighty has sent such tragedy upon me?"[9]

And David: "Do not abandon me, O LORD. Do not stand at a distance, my God. Come quickly to help me, O LORD my savior."[10] "Do not turn a deaf ear to me. For if you are silent, I might as well give up and die."[11]

The wish to die is almost inevitable in those whose bitterness is capping a volcano of rage toward God. I know. I've been there, although I was not tempted to self-harm as much as to give up.

Why bother? If God wouldn't heal me, if He had turned His back on me after all my valiant attempts to please Him, then I figured I might as well just quit. I certainly couldn't try any harder or be any better. I'd done all I could, and it wasn't enough. Or maybe He wasn't enough. Maybe all those words about His love were just campaign slogans, good for posters but not good for much in real life.

One Sunday afternoon, as I sat outside on our back deck with the ocean sparkling in the distance and my children napping in their rooms, I determined to figure out what eluded me. I'd keep reading and asking and seeking until I could reconcile what I'd heard about God's love with my new reality.

Every sentence seemed to confirm my suspicions—that God was not nice. In the gospel of Matthew, I encountered Jesus as an outspoken confronter of hypocrisy. But instead of seeing the truth in what He was saying, all I noticed was His not-niceness. He seemed harsh, even mean. People asked Him questions and He responded by pinning them to the wall. That bothered me. *He* bothered me, grating on my polite sensibilities of the right way to conduct relationships.

He rescued some and not others. Spoke kindly to a few and blasted many. Healed randomly without much more than a caveat to keep quiet about it. It didn't take long for me to conclude that God was not, and never had been, *good*.

In one grand display of incensed wrath, I lifted my Bible off my lap and threw it across the deck. The big, black, leather-bound book bounced at least once, then landed helter-skelter, ripped pages flapping in the wind. I was so mad, filled with the need to hurt Him for not helping me.

I sat there for a long time, looking at my abused Bible, my heart pounding, breaking, slipping away from all I thought I'd believed. What would He do to me now? Despair crept in, taking up residence where faith had once ruled. In that moment, I realized that I hated Him. I loathed the One I read about in the Gospel stories He Himself had sanctioned.

He had failed me.

Failed to love me enough. Failed to take care of me. Failed to keep those time-worn promises of the good, blessing-filled, wonderful life He owed me.

This Jesus was not worthy of my love. I would sacrifice and struggle no more. Not for Him.

He didn't care and neither would I.

All that anger left me limp with soul-depleting exhaustion. My temper tantrums had yielded nothing more than a sense of inner ugliness. My Bible-throwing display of fury embarrassed me. I no longer felt like the good girl I'd tried so hard to be.

And so I withdrew.

Already naturally introverted, I now became a recluse. The thought of being with people who might see the churning mess inside me was terrifying. I was afraid they would see the truth, that I was an angry, rebellious, blasphemous sinner. I wrapped myself in a cloak of self-pity and shut everyone out.

Still, I never missed a "quiet time" with God. Reading my Bible in the morning had become a habit for me. Ponderously, I trekked my way from beginning to end. Every morning, I carved out time to read my appointed chapters, checking off this regimented discipline from my to-do list. Even as I questioned God's goodness, my spirit simply could not doubt His existence. I obediently forged my way through the chapters, deaf to what He was whispering to my spiritual ears.

One morning, I happened upon the fifth chapter of James. I'd read it before, of course, but this time the words seemed to jump off the page.

"Are any of you sick? You should call for the elders of the church to come and pray over you, anointing you with oil in the name of the Lord. Such a prayer offered in faith will heal the sick, and the Lord will make you well. And if you have committed any sins, you will be forgiven."[12]

Should I try it? Did I dare? Could it be that all that stood between my failing hearing and full healing was prayer? Maybe I hadn't been healed because I hadn't asked in the right way.

When I approached Phil about asking the elders of our church to pray for me, he jumped on it. Relieved to see even the slightest hint that my prickly heart might be softening toward God, he made arrangements for the following Sunday—plenty of time for me to worry about what I'd set in motion!

And worry, I did. About what to say, how much to admit, what they would think of me if I dared tell the whole truth. I worried my way through the rest of the week, half wishing I'd never mentioned James 5 to my husband. My worries about what people might think meshed uneasily with my fear of a silent future. I knew this would be my last attempt at convincing this cold and distant God to heal me. And if He didn't, well, then I'd be done trying. Done pretending.

Done with God.

CHAPTER 4

The Beautiful No . . .

a story I didn't deserve

When the day came for what I'd come to think of as My Embarrassing Ordeal, I dressed with meticulous care. After all, if you're going to expose yourself to close-up scrutiny, risking others seeing a glimpse of the ugly truth going on inside, every woman knows that the least she can do is look her best. I wanted to look like I had it all together. The reality was that I was rapidly coming unglued.

Walking into that meeting with the elders felt a lot like walking into the principal's office. Not that I knew much about that; after all, professional good girls like me rarely see the inner sanctum of authority. I'd spent my entire life avoiding confrontation and conflict, staying safely under the radar of the heavies. *What,* I wondered, *was I doing here?*

The small room threatened to close in on me as I sat surrounded by men whose stature seemed to dominate the space. On one side towered Bill Dauphin, the high school wrestling coach, a man who emanated a quiet sort of stern strength. Next to him stood the ever-dignified Al Linder. Successful and intelligent, he had kids near my age. And Ron McClain, who spent his days counseling with the Scriptures open on his desk, helping broken people put their lives back together according to God's plan. Hurting people were his specialty.

But I wasn't one of those. I was a good girl. I hated being the needy one.

What, I wondered, *would these men think of me if they knew the rage simmering just beneath my skin?* I couldn't meet their eyes, I didn't want them to see the ugly truth about me. I knew I needed to be here. I needed to see if maybe God would hear the prayers of these righteous men and consent to heal my failing ears.

My husband stood nearby, but back a step or two. No reassuring pat on my shoulder. No way to hide the fact that this was about me, and my problem.

I felt alone and scared. Scared of exposing the tumult inside, scared of losing control if I dared to loosen the firm clamp on my raging heart, scared of what might happen if God didn't do what I so desperately needed Him to do.

Scared of a future of silence.

Before I managed to conjure up a reason to flee, Ron called us to attention, ready to begin the ritual we all hoped would heal me. The men moved to dip their fingers in a small container of olive oil as Ron explained the ancient custom referred to in James, the beauty of the symbolism between oil and the Spirit, of healing of the body and hope for the soul. Each of these spiritual leaders had been here before, reliant on God to do what they could not, watching and waiting with a hurting one.

Faith filled the cinderblock room as the men touched my forehead, my hands, my ears. They prayed with such passion, such conviction. They laughed out loud with the joy of asking, knowing He heard. Confidently, they cried out to Him to make it right, to touch my ears, to give me back all I had lost, to halt the encroaching silence.

Of course, God could heal me! Surely He would. No doubt shadowed their prayers. They'd come at His invitation to ask for a good thing, and they asked with unshakeable faith.

I *believed* God could heal me.

Belief, as I understood it, was never my problem. I had never not believed. After all, the One who created my ears could surely wave His magic wand over them, fixing all those damaged cilia that short-circuited my brain's ability to conduct sound. The Bible is filled with evidence of healing. I loved those stories, believed every word. I knew that God hadn't stopped working in this broken world, and that He still healed today—sometimes.

Several well-meaning people had spoken to me about needing more faith, as if drumming up intense emotional feelings and calling them "faith" would work a spiritual spell that would bequeath me the right to be freed from what ailed me. And I tried, I really did. Every time I asked God to heal me, I waited and wondered. *Would He do it this time? Had I said it right? Felt all the right feelings? Was my faith temperature high enough?*

Now, my mind moving in and out of the elders' conversation with God, I could hardly catch my breath from the panic of facing my future without hearing. What if God ignored them too? What if He wasn't listening?

The other half of me remained so caught up in the rise and fall of these men's confident prayers that I felt enveloped in the sense that something transforming was happening here, something not of this world.

Something I wanted. Something I feared.

Time stood still as all my worries and dread were laid at the feet of the One, the only One, who could do something about them.

With these friends who cared so deeply pouring out their heart-felt petitions for my healing, I couldn't hold back my tears. I didn't politely cry—I sobbed. For me, for my future, for my fears and failures and the foulness that was threatening to undo me. I wept as I had never wept before, soaking my blouse with my tears, pleading with God to hear these men, to do for them what He hadn't done for me.

With one last desperate effort, my soul begged God to hear me, to heal me.

Oh, God, help me!

When I couldn't help myself, when I couldn't be strong or good or right, when I couldn't find a foolproof set of rules to follow, a plea of naked dependence was all I could manage.

And in that moment, something shifted. Not in me; I sat in a pathetic heap, huddled over myself, knees drawn in, face in my lap. But I sensed the darkness dissipating, as if clouds were being rolled back. Like on a stormy day when suddenly streams of light break through black clouds. Now light peeked through, gaining brilliance until it streamed over me—a light so radiant it caused that dingy room and those fervent men to fade away.

I felt God's presence envelop me, compelling me to sit up. To forget, in an instant, all my fears. All I saw was light—brilliant, soul-lifting light.[13] For just that moment, everything else disappeared. No people, no sound, no sensation except that all-encompassing Presence.

I was terrified. At the same time, I was filled with the strangest sense of safety. Afraid, yet not threatened. The essence of His presence surrounded me with such unearthly power that it frightened me out of all my fears.

Then, as the murmured prayers of the elders reverberated in the background, I heard a distinct voice. A real voice. A voice so clear it made every nerve on my skin stand at attention. Loud and commanding. The voice that felled the walls of Jericho, caused the shepherds on the hillsides of Bethlehem to tremble, the voice that will someday roll back the sky and cause every single knee to bow low.

That voice.

I knew who it was, and I heard what He was saying. Just two words. Two words and my name.

It's okay! It's okay, Diane, it's okay . . .

Over and over, His words washed over me.

It's okay . . . it's okay.

I knew without the slightest tinge of doubt what He was telling me: He would *not* heal my hearing.

He would *not* intervene and do what I wanted. He would *not* give me what I'd begged for. He would *not* say yes to all our prayers.

His answer was *no*.

And in that *no*, a strange flood of hope filled me. Somehow, in some way I could not begin to understand, He made it okay.

How could the word I dreaded most sound so loving and gentle? How was it that all my horror of deafness was swallowed up in that irrevocable NO?[14]

The only answer that makes any sense to me is that I felt loved as I never had before. I was *experiencing* the love of God in a whole new way. I hadn't earned it, hadn't followed the rules, had, in fact, done so much wrong. I had knowingly and purposefully rejected Him. He had seen that, had seen me—the real, hidden me I'd kept cloaked from everyone else, and yet, "He lifted me out of the pit of despair, out of the mud and the mire. He set my feet on solid ground and steadied me as I walked along."[15]

All I wanted in that moment was to linger in that hallowed place. Reveling in His presence, my soul sang with the joy of it. Joy I had never known, intimacy with the One who made me for Himself.

It was okay!

I wanted to shout it out loud, to dance, to raise my hands in the stunned glee of knowing. I felt it, I meant it—*it was okay!* I was caught up in His beauty, warmed clear through by a love that melted my hardened heart.

I don't know how long I sat in the light emanating from His presence. Probably no more than a moment. But that moment seared itself so deeply on my soul that the memory brings me back to that place in an instant. A moment of holiest joy.

The light receded, but not the joy. I was still there, sitting in the same plastic chair, surrounded by the same men who had brought me to this sacred place. But nothing would ever be the same.

I would never be the same.

I left the room wrapped in a cocoon of wonder, knowing I hadn't been healed but not registering the implications of His refusal. In the vivid sense of *feeling* the love of God for me, all I could do was tuck in tight to His presence.

By the time Phil and I got the children fed and tucked into their beds and the baby changed and nursed and rocked to sleep that night, we were both too tired to talk. While Phil fell asleep almost instantly, I lay wide awake.

What had occurred in that room? What had I seen and heard? Was it real? Was I crazy?

All I knew was that I had walked out of that meeting full of bewildered joy, uncertain about what had happened or would happen, but sure that I had encountered God personally, dramatically, and intimately. I had, quite literally, seen the light. I couldn't explain it, didn't fully understand it, but I knew I'd seen a glimpse of what the psalmist called God's "robe of light."[16]

The next morning, I woke up much the same as every other morning. Since I'd lost the ability to hear the high pitch of the alarm clock, Phil nudged me none-too-gently and mumbled sleepy complaints about why in the world I had set it so early.

Rolling out of bed, I stumbled to the kitchen to make coffee, ignoring the dishwasher that needed emptying lest I wake the baby and lose my only chance for solitude. Nestling into a corner of the sofa, I dutifully opened my Bible. The words from the ascribed Psalm for the day shook me fully awake:

> I waited patiently for the LORD to help me, and he turned to me and heard my cry. He lifted me out of the pit of despair, out of the mud and the mire. He set my feet on solid ground and steadied me as I walked along. He has given me a new song to sing, a hymn of praise to our God. Many will see what he has done and be amazed. They will put their trust in the LORD, Oh, the joys of those who trust the LORD, who have no confidence in the proud or in those who worship idols. O LORD my God, you have performed many wonders for us. Your plans for us are too numerous to list. You have no equal. If I tried to recite all your wonderful deeds, I would never come to the end of them. You take no delight in sacrifices or offerings. Now that you have made me listen, I finally understand . . .
> (Ps. 40:1–6, NLT)

My ears Thou has opened . . .

I read it again as my heart began to beat wildly at the thought. *Could it be?*

Leaning forward, I hesitantly tapped my pen against the coffee table in front of me. Instead of the sharp rap I hoped for, a dull thud met my ears. I tapped harder this time, the muffled *thwack* barely registering.

Slumping in my seat, I was enveloped in disappointment. Nothing had changed. I couldn't hear.

Yet something had changed, something inside of me, something I couldn't analyze or categorize or control. I felt different this morning. Lighter, fuller, comforted by a strange sense of rest. I felt almost . . . *happy.* I couldn't keep down this emerging undercurrent of joy and connection. It was as if *He was there,* right beside me. The One I had heard and known in that glimpse of brilliance. I felt His presence beside me on my faded sofa, wrapping me once again in His light and love. I wanted Him to speak again.

Deep in my spirit, I again heard words, real words.

I am here and I want you to listen to Me.

I am giving you a gift. I am going to teach you to hear. But first you are going to have to learn to listen.

What followed was an experience so rich I could hardly contain the joy, yet so sobering I could barely hold back my tears. His words sounded, not sweet and soothing, but sudden and stern.

Like when, as a child, I had panicked in the middle of the street while holding my father's hand. I'd tried to pull away, certain that the car in the distance was coming to force me from the safety of my father's grasp, to hurt me, to run me over and do me in. But instead of leaning down to assure me that I was safe, my dad had tightened his grip until my hand hurt. He'd pulled me hard to the other side while sternly warning me to yield my terror to him. Rather than leave me to my fate, my dad had yanked me clear of danger.

Now, I sensed my heavenly Father right beside me, so palpable it seemed I could feel the warmth of His skin. He was unveiling Himself to me, just as He had to Job, who couldn't help but cry out his wonder: "I had only heard about you before, but now I have seen you with my own eyes."[17]

His voice was clear and compelling. My soul sensed that I was being pulled close into the place I'd longed for on all those mornings when waking up to yet another day left me empty inside. The timbre of His voice brimmed with the love of a father firmly pulling his daughter to safety, and I heard His message, just for me.

Diane, you have sat under some of the best teaching of this decade. You have been to wisdom-rich seminars about marriage and family and living My way. You have listened to some of the best of My servants, read books from My wise men and faith-filled women. You have studied and memorized My words.

Now it is time to listen! To listen to Me.

Now is when the rubber meets the road. This is the time to put into practice all you have been taught. Listen and do what I say.

I will be your teacher. I will guide you along the right way for you to go. I will help you and hold you close and see you through.

I will do this.

I will be with you.

Pen in hand, I scrambled to write it all down, these words of His. To somehow catch the intricacies of what He said. Not wanting to miss one inflection of His voice, I could hardly keep up as I scribbled the words onto paper. This was HIM! *God—my Father!* He was speaking to me and my heart soared with the joy of it.

I knew I was facing a decision of such magnitude that it would change the course of my life forever. He wanted me to practice a whole new dimension of my faith, trusting Him to teach and guide me in a way that would require me to listen with a new set of ears.

Would I follow Him and surrender with joy?

Sometimes surrender is a one-time act. But more often than not, God's servants must learn it over and over again. We learn to surrender incrementally, sometimes moment by moment. We are challenged to let go of what we want in order to give way to what God decides.

Most of us make a mess of it.

We want our way and we want it *now*. No over-the-top, out-of-the-ordinary, paradigm-exploding trials, thank you very much!

When I embraced Jesus as a teenager, I thought it was all about me—that Jesus loved me, that He would weave all things together to make my life full and smooth, that He had a wonderful plan all tied up in a beautiful package for me to unwrap like a good girl on Christmas morning. For me, what was "good and acceptable and perfect"[18] was a neat and tidy life that would chug along merrily ever after.

Now, I knew otherwise. God's invitation into a surrendered-to-Him life is a summons to trust Him without insisting that I see the big picture. To open my hands and say, "Have Your way with me."

We are in good company when we choose this servant stance. I see it in the stories of three Marys who chose this way.

There is the young, eager-to-please Mary, mother of Jesus, a good girl, who faced the humility of cultural shame in order to bear God as a baby, without benefit of a husband.[19] Her words resonate with sorrow overcome by surrender: "Behold, the bondslave of the Lord; may it be done to me according to your word."[20]

Then, there is Mary of Bethany, who sat silently at Jesus' feet while life hustled and bustled around her. A woman who chose to listen, to hear, to pause and find clarity in the midst of chaos even at the cost of her sister's derision: ". . . few things are needed—or indeed only one," Jesus said. "Mary has chosen what is better, and it will not be taken away from her."[21]

Finally, Mary Magdalene was there when the angel of the Lord rolled back the stone from Jesus' tomb and declared, "He is not here; for he is risen." Her announcement of all she'd seen that morning was met with obstinate disbelief by the disciples and Peter. Yet she'd proclaimed the risen Christ anyway, surrendering her dignity in order to obey.[22]

To choose surrender is to choose something better than control, better than the perfectly manicured life. To choose surrender and all the messiness that goes with it is to choose to sit at Jesus' feet in unfettered abandon, to hear and understand the *better* thing that each of us so desperately needs.

Christ surrendered His equitable prerogatives to His Master— His body, His relationships, His justifiable right to be treated in a certain way. Motivated by love for us, to be sure, but even more by His love for His Father, Jesus chose to suffer and die in order to gain what His Father wanted more than anything—*us.*

"Though he was God, he did not think of equality with God as something to cling to. Instead, he gave up his divine privileges; he took on the humble position of a slave and was born as a human being. When he appeared in human form, he humbled himself in obedience to God and died a criminal's death on a cross."[23]

I sensed His Spirit holding out the choice to me: Would I die to all I wanted in order to give Him all of me? Would I humble myself, give up my "right" to hear, and offer my body as a living sacrifice, just as Paul pleaded with his people?[24]

Now, with God's mercy melting the ice around my heart, I wanted to please Him more than ever. For the first time my reasons had nothing to do with me and everything to do with Him. I could not help but marvel at a God who would speak to a woman whose self-absorbed petulance had pushed Him far away.

His words began to resonate from a place I couldn't see. Different from my own noisy self-talk, His voice soothed my soul with words of wisdom and distinct direction. When He spoke, I was learning to lean in and listen.

More and more I would hear Him in the silence. And what I heard changed everything.

CHAPTER 5

Where the Rubber
Meets the Road . . .

a story of learning the hard way

My *heel tapped hard* to the staccato beat drumming through
my brain: *I've gotta get this, gotta get that word, got to get it
right!* My knuckles grasping the cold arms of the metal chair in
the bomb-shelter-like testing room, my whole body rigid from
straining to hear, I squeezed my eyes shut and listened with all
my might.

The very nature of an audiological evaluation is negative; the
audiologist is trying to determine what you *do not* hear.

The patient waits alone facing a small window behind which the
audiologist sits surrounded by equipment. First, listening through
headphones, the patient is instructed to raise her right hand when
she hears a sound in her right ear, left hand for her left ear.

People who are deaf in one ear can compensate and hear nearly
perfectly unless each ear is tested separately. If both ears seem
the same, the headphones come off.

The audiologist plays a series of evenly spaced beeps and bonks, whistles and tweets. When the patient hears a sound—any sound—they are supposed to click the button.

I waited like a catcher in the outfield, hoping to catch the sound. When I did, I jammed that button in my hand, triumphant—I got it! Then more beeps, long silence, nothing. When there are long stretches of no sounds your stomach clenches, knowing you are missing something.

Next, the audiologist plays a recording to test how well the patient can hear in the context of complete sentences. At least thirty sentences, each patterned the same: subject, verb, predicate. A too-smooth voice of a woman speaks simple sentences like, "The ice cream fell on the sidewalk."

As anybody who is losing their hearing will tell you—you always try to beat the test. Almost as if by trying hard enough, you can will away the deafness.

I leaned forward to guess, to fill in the blanks. It didn't take me long to memorize the list of compound words used to test my comprehension. Get the first half and I could figure out the second. *Sidewalk, toothpaste, airplane, girlfriend.*

Even though I knew that God had told me "No," He would not heal me, I still tried my best to beat the test every time. I would lean forward, holding my breath, going after the sounds in the headphones as if my life depended on it.

What no one knew—no audiologist or otologist, no study or past precedent—was how much longer I would be able to hear *anything.*

Because the doctors were still trying to find the cause of my downward spiraling hearing loss, I kept going back for tests. Lots of tests.

Massive doses of Prednisone, followed by a hearing test to see if the loss was abating.

No.

Exploratory surgery, followed by another hearing test to gauge the results.

More loss.

I took vitamins, herbs, purges, and antibiotics. The doctor prescribed a no-salt diet—anything to hold back the raging flood rushing me down the river toward deafness.

Nothing worked.

I was twenty-seven years old when my doctor tore a sheet of paper off a prescription pad and handed it to me: *The hearing loss of Diane Comer has been medically evaluated and the patient may be considered a candidate for a hearing aid.*

I couldn't look at him. Couldn't choke out words to fill the silence. I'd come dressed up for this appointment, as if exchanging my mommy uniform of workout clothes for a skirt and heels might somehow lend dignity to what I dreaded.

It didn't work.

More hearing loss meant facing the reality that those unsightly amplifiers I found abhorrent had become necessary. If I wanted to hear my children, if I hoped to have a coherent conversation with my husband, I had to go ahead with what the doctors and audiologist had been urging me toward for months—hearing aids. I carried that piece of paper out the door as if it weighed a hundred pounds.

When I'd first dragged myself to the doctor to have my ears tested, I was shown how hearing loss was categorized: *Normal, Mild, Moderate, Moderately Severe, Severe, Profound.* Over the months that followed, I'd seen my own hearing rapidly slide downhill on paper. Boxes checked *moderate* in September indicated that my discrimination of speech was 76 percent, which meant I was missing 24 percent of the sounds around me. Now, eighteen months and innumerable tests later, I scored *moderately severe,* my understanding of words dropping into the 50–60 percent range. This meant I was now missing nearly half of all words in a normal conversation. I could no longer argue that I didn't need to wear the ugly apparatuses I dreaded.

The clinic referred me to a hearing aid specialist by the name of Tak Katsumoto. When I first walked into his gadget-filled office, Mr. Katsumoto did a double take, craning his neck to look around me, as if searching for his real client. In all his years of fitting hearing aids, he'd never once dealt with someone so young. But instead of registering sadness, his face burst into a smile of delight!

Assuring me that he could help me hear better, he practically rubbed his hands together with anticipation. Later, he would tell me about his frustrations at fitting older people who didn't really want to do the hard work involved in hearing with the mechanical help of hearing aids.

My hearing loss was such that silicone molds had to be made to reach into my ear canals to direct amplified sound as far into my ears as possible, lest even the faintest sounds escape. A clear tube ran from each mold, over the top of the ear to the hearing aid tucked behind. The molds itched on hot days, clogged with wax in response to the constant irritation of plugged ears, and smelled terrible if I was less than diligent about cleaning them regularly. Hardly the kind of accessory a young woman wants to wear!

The day I wore my first hearing aids turned out to be a day to celebrate. With the flip of the switch, my world woke up! The sound of water running as Mr. Katsumoto washed his hands, the scratch of his pen. When Phil's voice roared at me across the room, I had to restrain myself from covering my ears. Wow! So much noise!

But hearing aids are not like glasses. Anyone who is nearsighted knows that glasses can correct most vision to a perfect 20/20. Get the prescription right, and the world comes into focus. Hearing aids, in contrast, simply amplify sound, like putting a microphone in your ears and turning up the volume. While donning glasses brings crisp clarity to someone whose sight is less than stellar, hearing aids bring mostly loudness. The clarity necessary for comprehension is often lost in the noise.

Because of the steep decline in my ability to hear the mid-tones, where human speech falls, and the severe drop in my ability to hear high tones, it was nearly impossible to amplify one and not the other. Without hearing aids, I could barely register some sounds—crickets or buzzers or a knock on the door—yet with them, I still couldn't understand words unless they were spoken clearly and distinctly and directed right at my face. Unaided, I could hear the car door slam from inside the house. Yet I couldn't for the life of me hear the alarm clock or make sense of my son's words as he sat beside me sounding out phonics on the page.

Hearing aids came to seem like an empty promise: all noise and very little of what I really wanted—to understand the words of my son, to enter into the flow of my family's teasing. With those flesh-toned things hanging behind my ears, I could hear, but all too often I still couldn't *understand*.

Still, I wore them. Every day, without fail, I plugged those gadgets into both ears, adjusting the volume to get rid of the inevitable screeching, and set about working to hear. Yes, hearing took hard work. In fact, it was exhausting. All that sound and so much confusion about what it meant—and a great deal of misunderstanding as a result.

I don't know how often I thought the kids were arguing and stepped in with fierce mom-ness to put a stop to it, only to be met by looks of surprise. *What,* they wanted to know, *was I so upset about?* Only to find that it wasn't bickering I'd heard, but laugher. And I wonder still how much I missed when my kids became adept at speaking softly so I wouldn't hear.

Driving was the worst. The clamor of three kids and a new baby in the minivan could send me into a tizzy simply because there were too many sounds coming at me too fast. The immense stress of my encroaching deafness magnified an already stressful season of life.

Shame was the worst part.

Shame when I impatiently bawled out my son for something I thought I'd heard but had in fact misheard. Shame when I couldn't figure out why my little girl was crying, couldn't hear through the hiccups and wails where she was hurt. Shame when I hadn't heard the baby waking up. When I finally did, she was red with rage, sure she'd been abandoned.

It wasn't supposed to be this way, this life I'd so looked forward to. Sometimes it seemed that instead of the warm and embracing mother I longed to be, I'd turned into Monster Mom: angry when I shouldn't be, oblivious of what I needed to hear.

Would this be the way my children would remember their childhood?

By the time Elizabeth was two years old, I could hear only about 44 percent of speech, which means I missed most of the sounds she made. What felt like not enough hearing one month seemed like luxurious sensory overload by the next appointment.

All the while, my MRIs continued to be normal. Bone conduction tests came back normal. I emerged after each test with *normal* contradicting my reality. If only the doctors could find a cause, some reason for this corrosion of the nerves in my head, then maybe they could stop it. Or at least slow it down.

What the doctors did explain to me was this: There are hundreds of thousands of microscopic, hair-like receptors called cilia that line the spiral-like cochlear nerve nestled right behind the ear. Those cilia transform the mechanical sounds that enter the ears into an electrical impulse that travels up the eighth bundle of nerves to the brain and, voila!—registers sound.

For reasons no test has been able to articulate, those cilia began to disintegrate inside my cochlear nerves. The sounds that should have stimulated hearing in my brain suffered a sort of short circuiting, leaving me with less and less comprehensible sound. My ears hear, but all connection is lost before the sounds reach my brain. Each section of the cilia that were being inexplicably destroyed left me understanding fewer of the words I so desperately needed to hear.

I continued to learn and grow, even to revel in the newfound intimacy God had bequeathed me in my brokenness. But my ears grew ever more deaf.

When Janna tested me, she seemed to understand the roiling, just-under-the-surface emotions that often left me white-faced and anxious. Nevertheless, as warmhearted as she was, she was not hesitant to confront me if she knew I was bluffing.

On one particular day, as I strained to hear her words and repeat them back to her (even if I had to make them up), she pushed back from her perch behind the glass wall that locked me into this place of tension. Making her way from her tower room crammed full of recording equipment, through the hallway, she unlocked my sealed space with a *hmph* of exertion. I straightened in my seat, pasted a smile on my face, and waved her in, like a princess in her throne room.

As she held the test results in front of my face, I could hardly hold myself erect. That graph paper, filled with *x*'s where sound registered and blank spaces where no sounds penetrated, caused all the peace created by my life-changing encounter with God to begin wobbling precariously.

God telling me He wasn't going to heal me was one thing—this free fall into deafness was quite another.

As Janna confronted me, I wanted to sob, to wail. *But I can do this,* I told myself. I *will* do this. With discipline and dignity, I swallowed my disappointment, shook off my panic, and pulled my pain in close.

Janna wasn't fooled.

"Diane, what did I just say?" she asked.

Feeling the heat of embarrassment creep up my neck, I searched for words that wouldn't come.

She looked at me like a teacher catching a naughty student passing notes in class.

"Diane, do not bluff!"

Her words hung between us in the suffocating room. I could feel my face flame. Caught in my fakery, I glossed over the awkwardness with banal chatter, mumbling and bumbling inane words to make up for my awkwardness.

She wasn't about to let me off the hook. She had a lesson for me to learn that day that would resonate in my soul for the rest of my life.

"Diane, you *must* be honest. When you don't hear what I'm saying, you have *got* to ask me to repeat myself. Do. Not. Pretend. Never, ever fake it with me!"

For added emphasis, she rapped her nails against my chart like a conductor striking her baton on a music score. I gulped back the tears threatening to stream down my reddened face and apologized profusely.

"I'm sorry, I was getting what you said . . . just missed the last few words . . . I understood almost everything . . . really, *I'm trying!*"

But Janna would have none of it. Pretending isn't trying, a lesson I would learn over and over again in the ensuing years.

Pretending is simply pushing away the truth to hide in thinly veiled obscurity. We pretend when we don't want to see. We pretend when we don't want to be seen, like when my children play hide-and-seek by covering their eyes. *If I don't look at you, you won't see me.*

But slowly, insistently, God was trying to peel my hands away from my eyes. To strip away all the pretense that peppered my responses and show me that what He wants from me is unadorned honesty. Janna's goal was to teach me how to use every clue, every advantage, every one of my remaining senses to make up for the loss of my hearing.

She wanted me to hear even when I was deaf.

She was adamant that I not learn sign language. Signing is for those who are born deaf and need to function within the deaf culture, she explained. For me, a woman whose first language was English, it would be too confining. I learned to read lips by staring at people's mouths while they were talking and trying to figure out what they were saying by the auditory clues I could still hear. I didn't even know I was reading lips until Janna pointed it out to me; like most people who gradually lose their hearing, it came pretty naturally, a means of coping. But because only about 30 percent of the English language is lip-readable, Janna coached me to pay close attention, to clue into a person's facial expressions—Happy? Angry? Perplexed?—and then to reconstruct conversations by using all the clues I could.

Like Janna, who demanded that I be utterly transparent with her so she could help me adjust to my hearing loss, God insists on that same artless transparency in order for Him to mold me into a woman of grace and beauty, a woman who listens and hears and knows Him down deep. No plotted out prayers. No hands raised in worship with fists clenched tightly in rebellion. No plastic response to reality.

To be real is to reveal the shabbiness of who I am today. All the worn down places, the fading beauty, the seams straining in all the wrong places. When I am honest—no bluffing or posturing or princess play—that is when God draws me in close and speaks to me of all I long to know. He fills my not-enoughness with all that He is, and I wonder why I ever tried to be more than I am.

I once listened as a woman described her "date with God." First, she told a roomful of women, "I do my hair and put on makeup in preparation. I want to meet God at my best . . ."

Are you kidding me? Meet my God with makeup on, lest He see me as I truly am? Most mornings I stumble out of bed in rumpled pj's, detangling my confused brain as I prepare my coffee as quickly as my sluggishness will allow. I drop things, read words backwards in that early morning drowsy dyslexia. My breath is rancid, goo catches at the corners of my eyes, I am a hair-gone-wild mess.

Through Janna's admonishments to stop bluffing, I began to see that God doesn't ask me to fix my appearance, outside or inside, to have an intimate encounter with Him. He knows me, and He loves me. Even when I'm a mess.

The only thing He absolutely requires from me if I want to meet Him face-to-face is honesty.

David, that sweet psalmist of Israel, knew all about bluffing. He lied and pretended his way through adultery, schemed to cover his tracks, and when he couldn't, he connived to have his lover's husband killed. But something broke inside when he was found out and confronted—not by a witness, but by a prophet.

To pierce David's protective armor, God sent Nathan, who told David the story of a wealthy man who had everything he needed. Yet when a guest came to stay with him, instead of dipping into his own vast herd of sheep for a hospitable meal, he grabbed a poor man's only lamb, one the man had "cuddled in his arms like a baby daughter,"[25] and slaughtered it for his guest. Indignant, David "burned with anger" and demanded that the rich man die for his injustice.[26]

But Nathan wasn't done. "You are that man! The LORD, the God of Israel, says: 'I anointed you king of Israel and saved you from the power of Saul. I gave you your master's house and his wives and the kingdoms of Israel and Judah. And if that had not been enough, I would have given you much, much more. Why, then, have you despised the word of the LORD and done this horrible deed? For you have murdered Uriah and stolen his wife."[27]

David responded by coming clean, falling on his face in deep repentance. "I have sinned against the LORD,"[28] David cried.

That's when he wrote one of my favorite Psalms.[29] He worshiped the Lord for His compassion, asking Him to wash his sins away and confessing his shame. He got real with God, trusting in full on faith that the God he served heard his cry.

Here's just one line of his song: "Behold, you delight in truth in the inward being, and you teach me wisdom in the secret heart."[30]

Truth in the innermost being.

That's what God wants from us: to stop bluffing and tell Him exactly what's going on in our secret depths. To follow the pattern of David, this man after God's heart, and pour out to Him all our brokenness and confusion. All those bottled up feelings that "good girls" hide lest we be found out and found wanting.

At the root of this ability to be real is confession—of sin—a lost art in this day of rehearsed worship and PowerPoint sermons.

Confession, in centuries past, used to be a regular practice in the church, a prerequisite for inclusion. James urged his congregation to "confess your sins to each other and pray for each other so that you may be healed."[31] The word *sin* in this passage means so much more than I'd bargained for: "Missing the true end and scope of our lives, which is God. An offense in relation to God with emphasis on guilt. An aberration from the truth, error."[32]

I've learned that when I confess my sins, my flaws, my guilt, and my failures to God, He takes the softest washcloth to my mess and bathes me in beauty. I lean into His warmth, breathing in the scent of Him, wanting more. From admitting that I lost my temper and shouldn't have spoken so derisively to my husband *again*, I progress to shedding all the pride and defensiveness that makes me prickly and resistant to soul intimacy. I shed the part of me that pretends to be perfect, the part that keeps missing the point of the cross, which is redemption. Not simply to wash me clean of my sins, as magnificent as that is, nor to protect me from God's wrath, as undeserving as I am, but to redeem me from all the mess my sin-infected DNA dictates.

Jesus went after me, all the way up that infamous hill called Calvary, for one reason: to bring me to the Father. "For Christ also suffered once for sins, the righteous for the unrighteous, *to bring you to God . . .*"[33] [34]

I love the story of the woman at the well.[35] Perhaps it's because she is so honest, and by nature I'm so . . . *not*.

Ever careful about what anybody and everybody thinks, I've tried on every color in the rainbow in order to fit in. But this woman dives straight into an encounter with Jesus in the light of day. She doesn't cower or pretend. The way I read the story, it seems as if she's had enough of men's demands and shows no intention of taking any more. In her day, to be addressed by a man—and a Jewish man at that—without introduction or permission, went way beyond the boundaries of propriety. Who does he think he is?

This unnamed woman swishes into the story with a swagger I envy. Where does she get that kind of confidence? Is it all a show, or is she genuinely sure of herself? She responds to Jesus' request for a drink of water with a question—or is it a challenge? "How is it that You, being a Jew, ask me for a drink since I am a Samaritan woman?"[36]

But it's the see-through vulnerability of her heart that intrigues me the most. In John 4, it sounds to me as if she is attempting to control the conversation, switching subjects abruptly lest Jesus get too close to her wound.

And this woman has wounds—deep ones. She's been married over and over again. In that time this probably meant she had been either widowed or abandoned over and over again. No doubt she's suffered gossip, arched eyebrows, murmured innuendos—and careful avoidance by those who fear her experience might just be contagious. This woman is a survivor. And I wonder what isn't written, what else went on, what abuse she's suffered to make her so seemingly tough.

But Jesus refused to politely avoid talking about this woman's agony. Instead, He faced her greatest fear and shame head on, urging her to do the same. He offered her the only hope that would fill her gaping soul—Himself.

"Jesus replied, 'If you only knew the gift God has for you and who you are speaking to, you would ask me, and I would give you living water . . . Anyone who drinks this water will soon become thirsty again. But those who drink the water I give will never be thirsty again. It becomes a fresh, bubbling spring within them, giving them eternal life.'"[37]

It didn't take long for this ill-used woman to get it. She was thirsty, parched for more than any man had ever offered. Her dissatisfaction had led her down a rugged path of self-destruction.

Jesus offered more.

Sometimes I wonder how her life unfolded after that encounter. I wonder if she was instantly transformed, or if she entered into a process marked by victories and defeats. I read myself into her story and think she had to have been angry at all she had suffered. Had self-pity weaseled it's subtle way into her soul? Did she blame God as I had?

I confess, I stumbled back into my default mode of pretending even in the middle of writing these words. Lost in thought as I relived my story, my eyes suddenly registered the time.

Oh my! What time did she say she'd be here?

I frantically rushed around tidying up breakfast dishes, wiping the sink as if no one ever eats here and no messes get made in the process. As if that fresh cantaloupe just magically appears heaped in sparkling bowls, no seeds slithering down the garbage bin, no sticky mess attracting flies on the counter.

I had to get everything right before the arrival of my new friend, one of those rare and wonderful women who always look younger than their age even if they've eaten too much chocolate the night before. (Which of course they didn't—or wouldn't. Ever.)

In spite of all God has taught me, sometimes I still hide my rawness, staging my life as if I have something to sell. As if it is me I am selling, and I'm attempting to market myself into a higher price range.

Who wants to be friends with Miss-Perfect-Kitchen, anyway? If I want to be close to Katherine, and I do, then I am going to have to let her see me as I am, and simply delight in the beauty of the gift of friendship she offers. No apologies or pretending my house is neater than it is or that I am better than I ever will be.

I draw comfort and insight from the psalmist, David, because time after time, he lays bare his struggling heart. In Psalm 18, David breaks out in a song of overwhelming gratitude to God for safely delivering him from his enemies.

He'd been relentlessly pursued by Saul and a host of warriors, just as I often feel relentlessly pursued by my own overwhelming enemies of self-pity and pride. Like me, David was tired of it, worn out and done in by the daily battle for survival:

> *The cords of death entangled me;*
> *the torrents of destruction overwhelmed me.*
> *The cords of the grave coiled around me;*
> *the snares of death confronted me.*
> *In my distress I called to the LORD;*
> *I cried to my God for help.*

From his temple he heard my voice;
  my cry came before him,
into his ears.

                    Psalm 18:4–6

Did David instantly know he'd been heard? Or were there months of pleading, hoping, wishing, begging for God to answer his cries? Did he moan about the unfairness of his situation? Did he demand that God rescue him? Did he spend hours and hours lying in the dark, wrestling with God, weeping and shaking his fist at the silence? Or like Paul, did David ask three times and then graciously give in?[38]

Somehow, I don't think so.

I think David wallowed, like I did, for a long time. I think his despair lingered on and on. During endless mornings of waking up to waves of heart-pounding anxiety, his chest heavy with the weight of his worries, I think David feared for his future.

I'll bet he blamed God, just as I did.

I was sure He had let me down—me, His good girl. He'd failed to be faithful, to watch over me, to give me the wonderful life He'd promised.

Why the pause between my cry reaching God's ears and His dramatic response? Was the silence my fault? Had I failed to drum up enough of that mysterious feeling called faith, as if by working myself into a frenzy I'd earn the right to be heard? Or could it be, as some say, that we must learn our lessons well before we're allowed out of the hurricane? That He is waiting, like a tyrannical teacher, for us to get it right?

Could that be why?

Or could it be that saying the right words, following a correct set of steps, or gushing all the "right" feelings has nothing to do with whether or not God hears us?

Sometimes, when I can't understand what someone is saying, I ask them to try again. To rephrase, to use different words, to clue me in on what they're trying to communicate. I look at their eyes, watch their face, read their lips, listen hard for the bits that will clue me in. I want to hear and understand.

Perhaps it's not the right words I need, but the right heart.

David, groping, struggling, failing, trying again, was having his heart changed through his own inadequacy:

"He reached down from on high and took hold of me; he drew me out of deep waters. He rescued me from my powerful enemy, from my foes, who were too strong for me."[39]

Why? David thought it was because of his righteousness, his faithfulness, his integrity and purity. He was sure his blamelessness and humility had something to do with it.[40]

I wasn't humble. I was filled with indignation that God had failed me. Hurt by His inaction, I placed every bit of blame on God. I was good, and I didn't deserve to be deaf.

Maybe that's why He delayed—not because He *wouldn't* hear me but because He *couldn't*. Maybe my good-girl self-righteousness filled up the space between His ears and mine.

Maybe He had to wait for me to be ready to change.

As Janna had confronted me about my lack of honesty during the hearing test, God began prodding me to take an honest look at my inner life.

I had been angry inside for so long, feeling intensely sorry for myself, that it had become deeply ingrained in my daily thoughts. Anger at God, anger at my circumstances, anger that God hadn't given me the perfect life I had thought I'd signed up for all those years ago.

When life goes bad and we stay mad, something terrible happens inside our souls. We lose our ability to hear, and suddenly God seems far away and silent. He won't answer back, won't coddle and console us in our fury.

This is why I cannot help but question the view I've heard bandied about with such impunity: *"It's okay to be angry with God."*

Really? Are you sure?

I'm not so certain. In fact, I think I was in a dangerous place when my heart was raging against Him, my soul teetering precariously close to the edge of that deadly cliff of rebellion. Crazy things happen when we willfully push away from the love of God, things that leave wounds and scars that can last a lifetime—mistakes, misjudgments, misery. Much like a child who inadvertently injures himself in a fit of momentary temper, I was working myself into a fury that could have caused irreparable harm.

That God can handle my anger, I have no doubt.[41] The problem, I have come to believe, is not with God, but with us.

Our souls are not strong enough to withstand the gale-force winds of intense and sustained anger. The roof is blown off, boundaries are broken, we are exposed to our own shocking ugliness. When that still, small voice of reason questions the rightness of our anger, we raise the volume, and sometimes we can't stop.

The spark that fueled my anger was intense self-absorption, which led to self-pity. And self-pity, I have learned, is a sin that keeps us away from God.

Until then, my regular forays into self-pity seemed rather benign, a girlish means of passively protesting what I couldn't control. But I was learning, through daily doses of listening with the Word of God open on my lap, a whole new way of thinking.

I was awakening to the idea that God had not so much saved me to make me better as to make me His. And not only that, but my me-centered faith had left me stuck with a whole lot of me, and not much of Jesus—a combination I was coming to see as repulsive.

Self-pity is subtle and circuitous.

Self-pity slips into relationships, strangling goodwill and preventing grace. More of the conflicts between my husband and me are started by "hurt feelings" (aka self-pity) than any other instigator. I feel bad for myself, and I think he should feel bad for me too. And then I think he ought to fall all over himself, making it up to poor little me. If I pout for a while, it's his just due. When I decide to indulge him by cheering up, I expect him to be ever so grateful for my renewed favor.

I believe that most of the *self*-prefixed words cause me to slide into sin: self-defensiveness, self-centeredness, selfishness, self-protectiveness, self-promotion. Any time I make my *self* the object of my (and everyone else's) primary concern, I am setting myself against God.

And that's not good. Not good at all.

When my audiologist pulled me up short by confronting me about my bluffing, she had no way of knowing she'd paved the way for me to stop pretending to God about just how angry and devastated I was. Or how her honest way of relating would usher me into hearing things I never could have heard as long as I stuck to the hunky-dory good life script I'd insisted on for so long. God was inviting me into a deeper place, a chamber only accessible through the hard-to-open door of guileless transparency. Not because I was good or pure or as a reward for doing right. I was broken and ugly and utterly helpless.

That is when He heard my cry. That's when He showed His love by seeing through to my true self, that part of me that longed to trust, to draw near, to experience Him in the rawness of real life.

On that morning when He told me it was okay *and* He wouldn't heal my ears, He actually rescued me from my own worst enemy: *me!* In that moment of spectacular grace, God rescued me from the mess I'd made for myself.

I didn't do it right. I wasn't a good girl. But in His mercy, He lit up my darkness.

He saved me from myself.

CHAPTER 6

Treasures in the Darkness . . .

a story of beauty in brokenness

Several years after my initial descent into deafness, my charts showed an inexplicable suspension in its progression. I couldn't hear any *better*, but neither did my hearing get much worse.

My team of doctors couldn't understand it. Mystified, they ordered test after test, trying to determine why my hearing loss seemed to be slowing down. They had no idea.

But I knew.

A short time after I'd yielded my demand that He heal me, I'd begun to wonder if I dared to ask Him for what any mother would want, what I longed for the most—more time to hear my children.

I knew better than to assume an attitude of entitlement all over again; to risk what I was gaining was out of the question.

Hearing God had become my passion, a reason to get up in the morning—the focus of my joy.

But every time I missed the stumbling sentences of my toddler or the whispers of my daughter or the boy-secrets too soon gone, my heart clenched in grief. A new baby now graced our family, the first to be born after my life-changing diagnosis. These precious lives were mine to know and mold and delight in—He had entrusted these gifts to me.

The importance of my role as a mother weighed heavily on my heart. How could I guide them deeper into relationship with Jesus if I couldn't hear their hopes and fears, their questions and concerns? If talking to me was too hard, wouldn't they give up and dismiss me as dispensable? How I longed to listen and hear them so I could know the nuances of who they were and who they would become. I was afraid that the rate at which my hearing was declining would preclude the possibility of shared confidences.

One evening as I walked along the shore of Seacliff beach, less than a mile from our home, with the sun hanging low to the west and my children romping and squealing and chasing waves, I asked.

Father, You know I'm Yours, all Yours. I really, honestly only want Your will, Your best, even if it's my worst. You know that, don't You? That I'm all in now, no conditions or expectations, no stipulations that You do for me what I'm asking . . .

But these children You've given me!

I look at John Mark and all his strength of will. I get this boy—how he's not going to stop asking questions and probing for answers until he gets at the heart of the truth. I want to be the one to hear him. I want to be that person who knows what he means by the inflection of his voice, the mother who understands no matter what.

And Bekah, my joy-filled sparkle of hope. She needs me, Father, I really believe she does. She can't decide if she's a people-craving extrovert or a thought-filled introvert. How I want to ease her through all the confusion ahead, to guard her when people try to exploit her beauty and her open-hearted friendship. Please, Lord!

What about little Beth, my quiet and content middle daughter? How will she learn to express those things I see hidden behind her eyes? She's my shadow, keeping herself close to me all day every day. How can I be her friend if I can't understand what she has to say?

And now this new one, Matthew. He needs me to talk to him, to hear his little boy silliness, to listen to his cries. How will he ever learn to talk to me if I cannot hear? Father please!

Will You slow it down, this loss? Give me a chance to raise these little ones, let me hear until they're old enough to walk with You. It's going so fast—can't You just hold off the inevitable for a little while?

On and on I walked, a strong sense of God at my elbow. I could almost feel Him thinking, as if He was considering my questions, weighing what He had in mind against what I was asking.

I heard nothing, but I felt His presence as we walked by the sea He had crafted with His own hands.

I could still smell the smoke from the fires of my own headstrong rebellion, and the stench left me wondering if the God I was getting to know would be merciful enough to grant the pleas of my mother's heart.

And so I asked in careful tones, not really waiting for an answer, just hoping. Wishing that the loss would slow down. Watching to see if this time He'd say yes.

Would God help me find a way to stay connected to Him, to each of my children—to hear their hearts if not their voices?

During the early years of my faith journey, I learned a new word. It was a word I'd never heard in my previous life, a word not exactly bandied about on the evening news.

Blessing.

People often use this word as a sort of endearment, their voices going soft and sweet and full of hope. The word appealed to my good-life-seeking sense of safety and dovetailed nicely with the wonderful life I'd signed up for.

A blessing, I believed, was all sugar and spice and everything nice—the day-by-day evidence that the formula worked: If I tried hard to live as a good girl should, then I would be blessed by God.

My parents had taught us to notice all the blessings in our lives. To make a gratitude list when life seemed hard and the road got bumpy.

Count your blessings, name them one by one, and it will surprise you what the Lord has done.[42]

And so I'd learned to count my blessings. To give God credit for the good, nice, loving goings-on in my life.

My definition of blessing looked like a perfect life where everyone is happy and healthy and has plenty of everything. I thought it meant a reward for a life well lived—sort of a carrot-and-stick philosophy. The carrot included all the protective blessings I thought God promised. The stick was His discipline if I chose to go against Him, the consequences I knew came with disobedience.

My definitions fit very well with my neat and tidy life. The problem was, my definition did not fit so nicely with *real* life. Or the Scriptures.

The word translated as *blessing* in the New Testament is derived from the Greek word, *makarismos,* which means "to be indwelt by God through the Holy Spirit and, therefore, because of His indwelling to be fully satisfied in spite of the afflictions of life."[43]

To be blessed actually means to be *fully satisfied.*

To thrive on the inside even if life is falling apart on the outside.

To be so filled with the joy of the Holy Spirit within that we are able to endure and taste the sweetness of His love even in the midst of bitter reality. Even when it hurts, even when we do not understand.

According to Scripture, this kind of blessing is unknown apart from God. No one can conjure it up or fake it for long. It is something God gives whenever we choose to fully entrust ourselves to Him.

James wrote, "Brothers and sisters, as an example of patience in the face of suffering, take the prophets who spoke in the name of the Lord. As you know, we count as *blessed* those who have persevered. You have heard of Job's perseverance and have seen what the Lord finally brought about. The Lord is full of compassion and mercy."[44]

God's definition of blessing is far broader and wiser and, to tell the truth, harder to swallow than the one I'd made up. It almost always includes suffering and the opportunity to choose God's way over my own self-protective tendencies to grasp for control.

James assumed that everyone remembered the prophets' lives as *blessed,* despite the fact that their histories record agonizing suffering.[45] Elizabeth called Mary blessed among women because she carried the son of God in her womb,[46] despite the fact that she would face certain rejection from those around her, not to mention the death of her child.[47] Mary considered herself *blessed*, even knowing that heartache would dog her footsteps.[48]

Not a whole lot of fairy tale endings.

I found myself continually reminded of Jacob's story in the book of Genesis. As I went about my days, caring for my kids, delighting in this strange new freedom, his story hounded me.

Like a burr caught on my sock, I couldn't seem to shake him from my thoughts.

Jacob and his twin brother, Esau, wrestled their way out of their mother's womb into a childhood of intense competition and frequent deception. Rivals from day one, these brothers were willing to do just about anything to latch onto what they wanted. And what each of them wanted was what was best for *themselves*.

Esau wanted freedom—room to roam, a band of brothers with whom to hunt and conquer, food when he wanted it, fixed how he liked it.

Jacob wanted ease—a warm fire, amiable conversation, enough extra to make life comfortable. More than anything, he wanted *more* than his brother had.

Their rivalry wasn't helped by their dad, Isaac. By the time the twins were born, Isaac was sixty years old and feeling his age. He openly favored Esau, born first by a hairsbreadth, simply for the stew his hunting skills put on his plate. In fact their family history reads like a tutorial in deception.

First, grandpa Abraham pretended to be traveling with his sister when the territorial king saw Sarah's beauty and wanted her for his own. Rather than risk his own neck, his fear led Abraham to risk his wife's well-being, watching from afar as she was led into the king's harem.[49] Isaac did the same when his wife, Rebekah, was coveted by a different king.[50]

Is it any wonder that Isaac and Rebekah spent the subsequent decades pitting their sons against each other? With sparse insight, the Scriptures note: "Isaac, who had a taste for wild game, loved Esau, but Rebekah loved Jacob."[51]

As they approach adulthood, Jacob and Esau seem bent on each other's destruction. When Jacob gets caught red-handed attempting to rob Esau of his promised blessing,[52] all hell breaks loose.

As Griffith Thomas, a preacher in the early 1900s, wrote: "Mortified at the loss of the blessing, and hating his brother on that account, Esau forms a resolve marked by cold-blooded calculation . . . he makes up his mind to kill his brother."[53]

Jacob runs for his life and ends up working for his uncle Laban, charlatan extraordinaire. For twenty years,[54] Jacob strives to get ahead, only to be set back again and again by the one man capable of outfoxing him.

When he falls head over heels in love with Laban's daughter, Rachel, who "had a lovely figure and was beautiful,"[55] he asks his uncle for her hand in marriage. He has to know the impossibility of such a request, given that the ironclad social norm of the time was to marry off one's children in order of birth.[56] But Jacob doesn't want Laban's oldest daughter, he wants the prettiest one. His uncle agrees and Jacob doesn't dare question his luck.

Somehow, perhaps due to free-flowing libations or a lack of proper lighting, Jacob fails to recognize the switch until the morning after. Instead of Rachel in his bed, he finds her older sister, Leah. And man, is he mad! Storming out of his tent, he rushes to confront Laban. "What is this you have done to me? I served you for Rachel, didn't I? Why have you deceived me?"[57] he demands.

Can you imagine Leah's reaction? Did she even know that Jacob was expecting Rachel? Had she lived in her beautiful younger sister's shadow so long that her new husband's revulsion when he woke to find the wrong sister at his side shattered her into a thousand pieces?

Truth be told, I've never much liked Jacob. He was the bad boy, manipulative and pushy, a liar and deceiver. But his repulsive reaction to his wife on the first morning of their honeymoon struck me as the ultimate meanness. I fairly felt her cringe, forever damaged by his rejection.[58] *How could he?* Yet over and over, God purposely identified Himself with this man: "I am the God of . . . Jacob."[59]

The God of *Jacob?* Really? What was it about Jacob that prompted God to promote him over and over again? To identify Himself with someone who seems like the epitome of perverseness? God comes across as doggedly emphatic when He commands, "Do not steal. Do not lie. Do not deceive one another,"[60] yet He stakes His name proudly to one whose very name means deceiver.[61] In spite of all Jacob's obvious failures and devious ways, God does not condemn him. What can that mean?

Jacob's messy saga continues with more rivalry, this time— surprise, surprise—between the two sister-wives, Leah and Rachel, each bent on outdoing the other in a wild race to see who can bear the most sons. The family grows to include four sons by Leah, who taunts Rachel for her inability to conceive. Rachel then insists that Jacob sleep with her servant in order to claim those children for herself. Two more sons are born. Not to be outdone, Leah, whose body seems to have become worn out from bearing all those boys, pushes her own maidservant into Jacob's bed. Two more sons follow soon after. Once more Leah gets pregnant. She bears two more sons, and then finally, a girl. Somewhere in there, Rachel conceives and has two sons of her own. Twelve sons and one daughter in all.

He's a busy man, that Jacob.

By this time Jacob is homesick. He longs for the days of peace and quiet in his mother's kitchen. Yet he's sure that his uncle, now also his father-in-law and the grandfather of his crowd of kids, will be none too pleased with the idea of his offspring migrating back to Canaan. So once again, Jacob slides down the slippery slope of deception to get what he wants.

Somehow Jacob manages to move his entire household and all its considerable paraphernalia before Laban finds out. Laban is furious!

"What do you mean by deceiving me like this? How dare you drag my daughters away like prisoners of war? Why did you slip away secretly? I would have given you a farewell feast, with singing and music, accompanied by tambourines and harps. Why didn't you let me kiss my daughters and grandchildren and tell them good-bye?"[62]

What a mess!

God intervenes by warning Laban in a dream to leave Jacob alone. After a heated argument, the two men come to an uneasy truce and Jacob moves on to face what he's terrified will be a mortal confrontation with Esau. But on his way, Jacob instead meets the only One he cannot deceive.

Jacob comes face-to-face with *God*.

For hours, Jacob wrestles in the dark with an unidentifiable opponent. All he knows is that he is being attacked and can't win. By dawn, he is wearing out, near the end of his strength, with a growing certainty that his opponent is no mere man, but God Himself. But instead of giving up and letting go, Jacob grabs hold of Him with his last remaining strength, striving to get what he wants: a blessing.

In the poetic expression of the King James version of the Bible, Jacob's declaration sounds like boldness tinged with bravado: "I will not let thee go, except thou bless me."[63] He holds on to God in an adrenaline rush of determination. He is desperate, single-minded, intentional.

Griffith Thomas opened my eyes to the truths imbedded in Jacob's story. "How like he is to many of us today! We do not realize that all these untoward circumstances, these perplexities, these sorrows, are part of the Divine discipline, and intended to bring us to the end of ourselves. And so we struggle, and strive, and fight, and resist, and all to no purpose. God has been trying to get Jacob to trust Him all these years."[64]

Had God been doing the same with me?

Trying to get me to trust Him with all my less-thans? To renounce my tendency toward a sort of spiritual subterfuge, afraid of being found out—afraid others would see that I wasn't the perfect woman I pretended to be?

How much easier it is to be a rule keeper, to parrot the principles and memorize the verses without ever having to bleed sorrow over my own raw heartache and subtle sins.

That, notes Mark Buchanan, "requires little or no personal engagement . . . you just follow orders . . . it need draw nothing from your heart, your mind, your strength, your soul. It's like paint-by-numbers: it requires no artistry, no imagination, no discipline, just dumb, methodical obedience."[65]

What I see now in Jacob is his daring courage to go after God. I read Jacob's story with edge-of-the-seat anticipation of his wrestling with God until he prevails and receives a blessing.[66]

For the rest of his life after his encounter with "the man,"[67] Jacob walked with a limp—a handicap, a less-than. Something most probably painful and most certainly limiting.

Jacob was done in and undone. Strengthened and weakened. Satisfied and made thirsty.

Something happened there by the river that forever marked him, bringing him to a place of surrender and redirecting all the pent-up passion that had tripped him up so many times before. Ultimately, Jacob joined the "poor in spirit"[68] of Jesus' acclaimed teaching from the mountain above Jerusalem—the sermon that "amazed" the crowds[69] for its controversial content: "God blesses those who are poor and realize their need for him, for the Kingdom of Heaven is theirs."[70]

This was becoming my story.

A good girl turned bad—a rule follower turned rule maker turned rule breaker—I'd mistakenly believed that righteous meant perfect, so perfection was what I strove for. Failing at that, I hid behind a mask of got-it-togetherness that wasn't authentic. I was a deceiver, hiding behind a cloak of pretense lest my badness leak out and someone see me for the fraud I was.

But all my fakery fled when I came face-to-face with the severe mercy of God. He loved me in all my brokenness. Not the me I pretended to be, not the me I wanted to be, but the me that I am right now in this moment.

Though the rest of his life did not treat him kindly, in the end Jacob became a listener.[71] And that is what I aspire to: to walk close enough to God to *hear* Him—not just words on paper, but the tone of His voice.

Even if it means limping my way through all the sounds I cannot hear.

My own suffering and failure marked the path straight into that place I craved. When the formulas that had always worked for me failed to answer my questions or satiate my thirst, I found myself finally ready to drink deeply of the living water—that thirst quenching, soul satisfying spiritual sustenance which all my rules could never give me:

To hear His voice and enter into His blessing.

The next years were fraught with challenges and frustrations, with increasing deafness and all the changes and adaptations necessary for me to cope. "Deaf aids" adorned my ears; I carried spare batteries in my purse; I had a special phone to enable at least some communication with my extended family far away.

My world was shrinking, but in many ways I was flourishing. Once the internal struggles that had kept me storm-tossed and battle-weary calmed under God's steadfast care, I settled into a spacious place of listening. The quiet became my sanctuary and my intimate meeting place with God.

Dallas Willard describes the still, small voice I have come to cherish and rely upon: "What is this still, small voice? The phrase is taken from the story of Elijah ... the translation might as well read, 'a whisper of a voice' or 'a gentle whispering' ... seemingly unremarkable, inconspicuous, unassuming and perhaps not immediately noticed."[72] He goes on to say, "In the still, small voice of God we are given a message that bears the stamp of his personality quite clearly and in a way we will learn to recognize."[73]

I can't find a tidy term to attach to this Spirit-shadowed listening I've learned to love. In airports and auditoriums, at parties and picnics, when the noise is too loud for my broken ears to take in, I burrow into the refuge of His presence. Inevitably, I find laughter there. It draws me in, this holy levity, my always-too-serious side delighted by His joy. More and more I hear Him, and He brings about the balance I need to bear up under the weight my deafness brings.

Because it's still there, the isolation.

Surrounded by people, I often feel all alone.

Deafness is an invisible wall that can seem impenetrable. I want out of this prison, want to break through that wall I cannot see, smash it to bits.

And yet I do experience blessings. Because I was losing my hearing, I had to learn to listen so much more intently than I ever had before. Casual conversation was lost to me, but between lip reading and watching expressions and hearing enough to get the gist, I could often hear through to what people were *really* saying.

In that place of listening, I seemed to gain a sense of what their souls most needed from God.

The first time I discovered this seemingly intuitive way of hearing was quite by accident. With growing anticipation, Phil and I looked forward to Cliff Barrows visiting our church in Santa Cruz to speak at our Christmas banquet and Sunday services. My husband had long revered this man for the impact his worship ministry had on not only evangelist Billy Graham's ministry, but on the church far and wide.

I dressed with care that evening, my children "helping," as I gently eased my toes into the sparkly nylons I'd purchased for the occasion. My favorite dress, a deep emerald green silk, slipped elegantly over my shoulders. To the delight of my daughters, I added layers of feminine loveliness: pearls hanging from my ears, dangling on my wrist, and roped around my neck. Everything was perfectly in place as I kissed my little ones goodnight, leaving them in the care of a friend. The relief of wearing something other than my mommy uniform of sweat suit and Reeboks energized me as I stepped into the night, looking forward to an elegant meal with treasured friends.

Shadowbrook, one of the area's finest restaurants, was nestled into a canyon at the bottom of a cliff overlooking the quaint seaside town of Capitola. An ancient-looking trolley carried patrons from the parking lot topside into the mysterious depths of the restaurant below. Eight of us stepped into the trolley that would ease us down the steep incline: Cliff Barrows and his beautiful southern belle wife, Billy; our pastor, and his wife, both elegantly clad for the occasion; another pastor-couple; and me and Phil.

My heart fell with the trolley when all I could hear was the clanking and grinding and shifting of gears that carried us to the restaurant. Everyone else chattered on as I waited for the noise to subside, wishing I could yank out my hearing aids to stop the horrible screeching that seemed to pierce right through my brain.

The round table we were seated at in the middle of the room wasn't any quieter. People talking, china clinking, silverware beating to the staccato rhythm of the music playing in the background—I couldn't hear a thing above all that noise!

Embarrassed, I nodded my head and pretended to listen, resisting the urge to cry. Lips moved, friends laughed, hearts and vision and wisdom were shared as I sat silent. When Cliff, ever gracious, looked across the table and asked me a question, I wanted to disappear under the table.

"Pardon me?" I asked, palms sweating, as I leaned forward to hear. But I couldn't make out what he was asking the second time either. Flustered, feeling foolish, I swallowed down the awful grit of inadequacy and said, "I don't hear very well. Can you repeat that?" My pastor and friends around the table looked on in embarrassed sympathy at my understatement.

Somehow, the conversation flowed again after that awkward lull, leaving me alone with my thoughts.

This is awful, horrible. What am I doing here? I want to hear! God, what were You thinking? There can be no good in this, no good at all.

And that is when His voice brought me in close.

"Diane, you can pray."

Here? Now? But we're talking . . . or at least they are. And I can't hear what they're saying. I just want to go home.

My whining sounded pathetic even to me.

His silence said more than words ever could. I felt, rather than heard, His urging—that compelling way of His that makes me want what I didn't know I needed.

Slowly, understanding dawned: *I am here to pray. That is His assignment tonight. He isn't feeling sorry for me, not at all. He wants me here for this reason.*

Humbled and validated at the same time, I sat up straighter, leaning into His Spirit to listen for those elusive words, beginning to understand that He wanted me to spend the evening focused lovingly on these people around the table, praying for them.

Under a sparkling chandelier, with candlelight and white linen casting an ethereal glow, I turned to one person and then another, asking Him what to pray for. With God Himself as my guide, I began to learn a way of praying I'd never heard nor heard of, something uniquely mine and beautifully His. It was as if we were praying together, my Lord and I.

Jesus, seated right next to the Father, with the Spirit hovering close, was inviting me into their conversation about people they loved. In tandem, it seemed, we spoke blessing over each one. I saw these people as He did, wonderfully and intricately complicated, mercy-washed and clean. I had no knowledge of their deepest fears or burdens or troubles, but He did . . . and so I just blessed each one.

We blessed each one.

As they laughed, we laughed with them, me having no idea what delighted them so but loving the way their faces lit up with joy. The evening was holy and filled with more wonder than I could take in. My ears heard only raucous noise, but my spirit heard everything He said. No longer mourning, my soul danced with God.

I think the apostle Paul learned how to pray in this way. He seemed to know exactly what to ask for his people. While his letters were pointed and practical, many times he paused to let them know he prayed for them. Lyrical poetry flowed from his pen as he wrote his prayers for the people he loved.

To the Philippians, he wrote: "I thank God every time I remember you. In all my prayers for all of you, I always pray with joy . . . being confident of this, that he who began a good work in you will carry it on to completion until the day of Christ Jesus."[74]

And to the Thessalonians: "We always thank God for all of you and continually mention you in our prayers. We remember before our God and Father your work produced by faith, your labor prompted by love, and your endurance inspired by hope in our Lord Jesus Christ. For we know, brothers and sisters loved by God, that he has chosen you . . ."[75]

And passionately, to the Ephesians: "When I think of all this, I fall to my knees and pray to the Father, the Creator of everything in heaven and on earth. I pray that from his glorious, unlimited resources he will empower you with inner strength through his Spirit."[76]

To pray with Jesus for His people has brought a new dimension to my listening to God. This praying, talking, singing, laughing, *being* with Him is what He offers to each of us. But it's not easy to hear Him. It takes determination—a Jacob-like tenacity to keep at it, to ask and seek and knock over and over and over again.

As A. W. Tozer wrote, "He waits to be wanted."[77] He waits until we want to hear from Him more than we want to communicate with anyone else—more even than our own people. Then He invites us into an ancient sacred grove of towering quiet and gives us gifts far greater, treasures in the darkness: wisdom, singing, joy, purpose.

This is how He came to me in my flustered limitations, this is what He offered instead of keen hearing and vivid conversation. I have found that this listening-asking kind of praying is more like a whispered knowing between intimate friends. There is nothing laborious or pious about it. I rarely go to my knees; mostly I am folding laundry and listening. Or walking and listening. Or sitting through another sermon I cannot hear and listening.

Though He has never let me hear anything even remotely prophet-like, and no science fiction—style mood music plays in the background, He gives me the knowledge that we are praying *together*—praying and delighting in someone He loves. I have the delicious sense that this entwining of His Spirit with mine makes a difference I will not see until I meet Him face-to-face.

Once, during a run in the Oregon rain, when I was lamenting my inability to pick up the phone and call my children, now adults, He drenched me with words intended just for them. He gave me a word for my firstborn: *Shalom*. I knew this was what he needed, not because I knew why, but because the Spirit said, *"Shalom, pray shalom over your boy."*

Then, on through my list, faster than I could scribble onto a scrap of paper in my pocket, for each one He gave a word, a phrase, a snippet of knowledge. Like Paul knew how to pray for the Colossians,[78] people he'd never met, never talked to, never heard from, I knew how to pray for my children.

I don't need to be able to hear on the phone to know what a mother longs to know, because He does. And now I pray not from the earthly worries of motherhood, but out of a wealth of wisdom from the Spirit who watches over my children when I cannot. The one who calls Himself El Roi, the God who sees.[79] The One who allows me to hear His words, to see and know beyond what my dear ones could ever tell me themselves.

My greatest fear—that my children wouldn't want to do the hard work of talking to me as I grew deaf—was never realized. They did talk to me. A lot.

When my youngest son wrote in his graduate school essay, "My mother has always been a close friend to me. She is one who I go to for advice often, with no fear of judgment," I knew the Father had bent in close to hear my cry on the beach so many years before.

This is what I know now that I wish I had known all those years ago: that faith, real life-changing, world-impacting faith, has nearly nothing to do with turning my suffering into a sales pitch to get people to sign on the dotted line of evangelical Christianity. Nor is it about following the rules and thus becoming a beacon for goodness in God's marketing campaign.

Real faith, the kind that redeems the me that I am, the kind my own people can touch and see and grab hold of, happens when I believe—when I honestly *know*—that God is good in the midst of my suffering and has a purpose for me even in my brokenness.

My own faith failed, not when I questioned God's power to heal me, but when I doubted His goodness at the deepest level because He chose not to heal me. I have been humbled, deepened, chastised, and charmed by His bringing me close to whisper sweet wisdom into my broken ears.

And now I wake each day knowing there are treasures yet to discover—so many more joys yet waiting for me as I entrust both the good and the hard to Him.

CHAPTER 7

Leaning In . . .

a story of letting go

To lose one's hearing is to lose control.

Being hearing impaired is often inconvenient and frequently isolating, but it can also be inherently dangerous.

On a walk down my street, even with my hearing aids, my ears fail to pick up the sounds of a car coming behind me. Out of nowhere, it seems, a five thousand—pound vehicle hurtles past, leaving my heart beating wildly. I didn't hear it, didn't know that inches from my elbow, potential calamity came too close for comfort.

All around me, the world is swooshing, screeching, honking, roaring, warning me to beware. But sounds that should come easily to my attention don't. I see movement, but not the noise that should accompany it. My eyes scurry to keep up with the random suddenness of sounds. Often, I simply cannot register the significance of what my ears fail to hear.

Most of what I miss by not hearing isn't so much dangerous as it is just a hassle. I try to do too many things at once and end up leaving the water running in the bath too long. I'm oblivious to the kitchen smoke detector that's trying to tell me my pan is smoking up the house or the buzzer meant to remind me to take the pie out of the oven before the crust scorches. I've had to do my share of fixing and scrubbing and throwing away things that are ruined because I couldn't hear the warnings.

During the early years in my ever-quieting world, surrounded by an impenetrable buffer that left me painfully aware of my unawareness, I wanted to hide. I couldn't hear, but I could see. The all-too-obvious looks from people who tried to talk to me in public, when I knew they were saying something but I couldn't figure out what, left me feeling exposed and inadequate. Staying home, where I had a greater sense of control, was tempting.

Yet I knew that to confine myself to an ever-smaller bit of navigable territory could not possibly be God's plan for me. I wanted to be courageous, to trust God in spite of my circumstances. I wanted my children to know what I was discovering: that He could be trusted, even when the going is hard.

Sometimes, I ventured out alone. Without Phil at my elbow to hear for me, without a friend to make my way easier, I gradually learned to say yes, to choose not to use my lack of hearing as an excuse to cower. I cannot say I like it, even now. In fact, when I'm navigating noisy crowds, I feel the loss of my hearing most acutely. Often I feel lost, overwhelmed by what I know must be making all that raucous sound but for me isn't making sense.

But oh, how I have learned that Jesus takes care of His lost sheep.

One time, I was waiting to board a flight from Los Angeles International Airport when the noise level began to rise suddenly.

Unlike everyone else, who could understand what was being blared over the loudspeakers, I stood in the middle of all that volume, bereft. What was I missing?

When a public venue is quiet, I might hear a word or two from a public address system—enough to alert me to the need to seek out the information everyone else is hearing. Normally, I'd find my way to a counter and explain that I cannot hear. But on this day, the counters were swarming with people clamoring for information. Lines were forming, but I had no idea why.

My heart began to beat faster and faster as I assumed there must be an emergency. My mind jumped to bombs and sabotage, terrorists targeting LAX. Frantically, I raced to the electronic board for departure information, hoping to read something, anything to explain what was going on. My eyes filled with tears of frustration, of fear, of the sheer overwhelmingness of not knowing.

As I stood in front of the blinking board, seeing every flight canceled, the weather outside typical Southern California perfect, I cried out to God.

What is wrong, God? I can't hear, I don't know what to do. Who can I ask? Help! Please!

Will You hear for me?

At the same moment I was calling out to Him in panic, a woman bumped into me. Or I bumped into her. I'll never be sure, since the halls were seething with a mass of moving people, hurrying to get nowhere. I turned to apologize, my words dying on my lips. I knew this woman! A tiny, sparkly-eyed woman who goes to our church, Adeline had often offered our family coveted passes to get into the Nike employee store in Beaverton. I knew her as a warm, welcoming woman always eager to help. Out of all the thousands of people stuck in one of the largest airports in the world, I had collided with Adeline!

Without a word, we clutched each other, both crying, both needing the comfort only the other was equipped to give at that moment. I needed her ears to help me know what to do; she needed my arms to hold her in her grief after arriving home from Indonesia, where she'd just buried her mom.

We stood in that crowded corridor-turned-cathedral, worshiping a God who had heard my plea for help and her sorrow.

He bumped us into each other at just the right time to tell us both, in clearest terms, that His love pours out, unhindered, even in the worst of times. I will be telling this story for the rest of my days, how "I love the LORD because he hears my voice and my prayer for mercy. Because he bends down to listen, I will pray as long as I have breath!"[80]

When we finally recovered from melting all over each other, Adeline led me to a corner, knowing I'd hear better away from the middle of all the chaos. The roar was such that I needed to get right in her face, too close for comfort, to read clues from her lips. She enunciated clearly, spoke louder than her Asian sense of propriety called for, took out a scrap of paper to write the words I wasn't getting. By listening hard and stringing the clues together, I discovered that nearly all the flights had been canceled due to some sort of glitch in the satellite system that governed flight control. All hotels near the airport were, by this time, booked full.

Adeline led me to a counter, elbowing her way to the front, intent on helping me. "She's deaf, she needs help!" In spite of her small stature, Adeline's love for me as a sister and fellow Jesus follower gave her a command no one seemed to want to mess with. My ticket was taken and changed without question for the earliest flight the next day.

My guardian angel then called my daughter over the roar, managing to get the message through that I needed to be picked up. I'd wait in front of the farthest baggage claim exit until Rebekah could make her way through the mess. And just in time, for Adeline's flight was leaving, one of the last to get through. Hugging me tightly, she rushed to her gate, both of us in awe that He had heard us in our respective places of distress, that even when we cannot listen, He knows.

I have learned that one of the surest ways to hear God is to let go of control.

Either by design or because all illusion of control has been ripped away from my grasping hands, the One who calls Himself my shepherd steps close when I've lost my way. He is near. And His nearness is all I need, all that really helps when life is not what it should be.

I cannot control the world around me.

With my sense of hearing diminished to such a devastating degree, I can't even pretend control. Is there risk in a deaf woman gallivanting around the world without help hovering at her side? Yes. Yet I dare not let my need for control hold me back from living my life fully, from pursuing relationships and adventure, from all the messy unsafeness that comes with being a woman who loves wholeheartedly. I don't want a life filled only with safe decisions.

I didn't want my deafness to hold my loved ones back from all He had for them, either. Which is why, when Phil came to me with his eyes full of excitement over an impending job offer, I hunkered down to listen.

Our first date had been to hear an evangelist speak at Mt. Hermon, a retreat center in the mountains of Northern California. Luis Palau was a man whose sold-out faith intrigued both of us. His passion for people and for his God-given mission to preach the gospel to the whole world stimulated within us a desire to follow God fearlessly, as he had. So when the Luis Palau Association began reaching out to Phil with queries about becoming the worship leader for English speaking events, Phil was so excited he could barely stand it. The thought of traveling around the world, leading worship, planning the programs, managing the millions of details that go into producing an out-reach event, seemed like a dream come true for Phil.

But for me, all that travel meant a lot of alone.

Phil would be gone for weeks at a time, out of reach and unable to help me navigate my already challenging life. The thought of sleeping without any sound to alert me to trouble left me weak with worry. Could I do this?

Saying, "No, you've got to stay home and take care of me," seemed like the worst kind of selfishness. My practical questions segued into faith questions: Could God do this through me? Could I trust Him?

My children watched, wide-eyed, as we talked endlessly about the opportunity. They knew how much I depended on Phil to help me do the things hearing people take for granted. He made all my appointments for me, explaining that his wife was hard of hearing and couldn't use the phone. He watched over me in church, clueing me in to what people were asking, making sure I caught the thread of conversations, answering the waitress's queries when we went out to eat. How would I handle emergencies or even just everyday challenges of functioning in a hearing world with Phil gone and out of reach?

One by one, these children, given to me from God, stepped into the conversation. They were offering to be more than most children ever have to be to their mom. First, John Mark, then in high school, spoke up.

"I think you need to do this, Dad. I'll help Mom. I can watch over everyone while you're gone," he said.

I saw a glimpse of the leader he was becoming as he pledged to step in and step up. Then Rebekah chimed in, listing all the ways she could help, her extroverted enthusiasm making it seem like the most wonderful adventure in the world.

Little Elizabeth, self-conscious and contemplative, took a while to be sure, but the day she came to us and said, "Daddy, we'll be okay. God will watch over us," was the day we decided. Indeed, God was calling all of us into this new adventure of faith. Even Matt, still a toddler, would be called upon to step in and help his mom as he grew older.

And they did, every one of them. My kids became so attuned to what I couldn't hear that they often answered for me. But it wasn't always easy for them.

Elizabeth remembers the angst of standing in line at the grocery store and watching me tense up, seeing me lean in closer to the clerk, straining to hear. Before electronic registers displayed the total as most do now, the clerks would sing out the amount I needed to pay, raising their voices slightly over the hubbub of clanking cans and the rattle of paper bags. They would try to make small talk with me while all I could do was nod my head and hope I wasn't making a fool of myself. I would often look down, fiddle with an imaginary something in my purse, cross off items from my grocery list. How do you explain to the salesperson that you can't understand a thing she's saying, what with the music blaring, the loudspeaker squawking, and too many people talking at once?

A shy little girl herself, Elizabeth often had to be my ears, stepping in to rescue me from a conversation I couldn't understand. At an age when all she wanted was to hide behind me, she had to push out front. Now, she says God used those experiences to push her out of her shell, that my handicap forced her to learn better people skills and confidence. But what mother wants to be the reason for her child's hardship, no matter how much good came out of it in the end?

The real failures go a bit deeper, exposing the ugliness just beneath the surface in those times of testing.

Phil was gone on a long trip overseas. He would have to miss our son's birthday, which fell right in the middle of a summer schedule that didn't allow much time for vacation and all the fun he usually brought to our family of six. Instead of staying home, I decided to pack up the whole crew and make the twelve-hour trip to the mountains where my parents lived. I was nervous. We didn't have a cell phone back then, and our van was showing its age. It would be a long drive without relief. But the thought of staying home with my kids, bored and with nothing to look forward to, tempted me to try it. Besides, I knew that as soon as I got to that refuge high in the Sierras, my kids would relish their freedom, and I would relax with my mom and dad to help.

We set off early, hoping Matthew would go back to sleep. But he didn't, and the children were restless and squabbling. Trying to manage four bored kids while weaving around I-5 truckers and stopping at every roadside restroom for my potty-training toddler was doing me in. By the time we made it to the Oregon border, over the Shasta mountain range and down through the scorching heat of the Sacramento valley, I'd reached the limit of my endurance. The van was heating up, and so was I. I could not figure out what they were fighting about or who was at fault.

At the same time, strange lights were blinking on the dashboard, and I was growing ever more worried that we'd soon be one of those cars stuck on the side of the road. My internal temperature heated to boiling just outside of Redding, California. That's when my daughter remembers, "You lost it. Yelling over us, threatening. You'd just had it. You pulled over to the side of the freeway and sobbed over the steering wheel."

All the fun our adventure had promised just a few hours before turned into fear. Mom was afraid and suddenly they were, too. As Elizabeth said, "You can bet we were quiet after that."

I feel the shame even now, wish I could erase the memory of a mother on a rampage. Every mother gets mad. Most mothers "lose it" at some point. For a mother trying to do life without hearing, the weight can sometimes seem unbearable. I was learning to rely on God, but it seemed that most of my learning followed close on the heels of failure.

It wasn't all sadness, though. My children grew up watching me struggle, sensing the yawning gap between what my ears heard and what my brain managed to decipher. And in that daily difficulty, they watched God step in to hold me close.

In the silence of my early mornings, before the house wakes up, before phones twerp and vibrate and insist on attention, I pad out to my favorite spot for listening. I make myself a pot of steaming tea and burrow into my favorite blanket in the corner of my big puffy chair. Balancing my cup on my lap, I sip and listen. I wait, quieting my spirit, temporarily ignoring my agenda for the day. I open my Bible to where I left off the day before and still my soul to hear.

That's where my early-rising firstborn knew he would find me every morning, filling my journal with words heard from God in the silence. That was my place of refuge from the hurt of not hearing, and I welcomed my children in.

In each of them, a hunger grew to know the peace they saw in my corner. God met me there, and they saw it as only children can, as the most real thing about me. In spite of all my flaws and failures, or maybe because of them, they saw the grace of God at work in their mom.

But John Mark also remembers fear. He was five when I was first diagnosed, and he saw the devastation. He remembers, more than once, seeing me come home from a doctor's appointment, unable to hold back my tears. He heard the conversations, knew the prognosis, and he was afraid. Would he lose his mother? Have to learn a whole new way to communicate in order to be heard? Now, as a father himself, he looks at his firstborn and realizes the load he quietly carried, tucked tightly inside. I do too, and I weep real tears of regret that I couldn't take it away.

God didn't promise that losing my hearing wouldn't hurt.

Rather, He assured me that He would be with me in the hurt.

He was with my family as well, letting them see His work in me. They watched my suffering, and one by one chose to identify themselves with the One who spoke into my silence.

Maybe that is the greatest gift of all—four kids, grown now, all going after God with passion and purpose.

Not because I was perfect, but because they saw that He is.

My children learned early on how much I needed time alone with God. Taking in His words of hope and love, correction and direction, is an essential ingredient of walking close to Him. They learned from me and from their dad that if they value God's Word enough to tuck it into their minds, chewing and relishing the truths they find there, He will "bring it to mind" by breathing its relevance into their daily lives.

I've seen this so many times in my husband, I've come to expect it. For every year that I've known him, Phil has read his Bible from cover to cover. He starts in Genesis on January 1 and ends his dogged trek the following December 31.

Every year.

For him, the surest way to hear God is by sticking his nose in His book and breathing it in, inhaling the scent of Him in every story, every letter, every tidbit of wisdom. Thus, when a quandary comes up—a problem that needs solving, a relationship that is confusing, a difficult decision—Phil inevitably quotes something he's read. Faster than he can figure out a response, the Spirit reminds him of what his mind is filled with: Scripture. A verse, a phrase, sometimes just a truth that sends him on a treasure hunt for "that verse on the right side of the page, somewhere near the bottom."

Our favorite go-to verse while raising our four children was James 1:5, "But if any of you lacks wisdom, let him ask of God, who gives to all generously and without reproach, and it will be given to him." (NASB)

And in those less-than-clear teenage years, we often clasped hands and cried, "We do not know what to do, but our eyes are on you," a battle cry right out of 2 Chronicles 20:12.

We savored the joy of hearing, of knowing beyond any doubt that this was *Him*, His imparting of the wisdom we needed and didn't have.

This is how God speaks!

Shama is the word for *hear* in the Hebrew Torah.[81] It means to hear, to listen, to obey.

To listen with the intent to obey.

Every day, when I take my dog, Jackson, on a walk, I see this in practice. As soon as I get his leash, he starts showing his eagerness to go with me in the manner of all master-pleasing hounds. Once I've gathered all my gear—waterproof jacket with hood, gloves, wicking socks, billed hat to keep the rain out of my face (can you tell I live in the Pacific Northwest?)—and venture out the front door, Jackson is smiling in pure dog-joy. If I forget something and need to head back in, he sits stoically waiting, frozen to his self-appointed spot outside. As we walk, he leans just a little into his leash, that boundary settling him into a place of security, of rest in the midst of moving forward.

It is when we come to a crossroad that he shows me what it means to listen. Ten yards from any potential turn, Jackson begins to glance back at me. Every few steps, he looks at me, then back ahead. By the time we reach the turning point, his head is swaying back and forth, nose stretched forward, sniffing, listening, looking for hints from me about where I want to go. His normally floppy ears perk high, twitching like a radar honing in on an exact location. If a dog could frown in concentration, he does. And when I finally shift direction, he's so attuned to me that we seem to turn simultaneously in perfect cadence like marines on parade.

Watching Jackson reminds me that "I want to have ears so tuned to the Voice that when God speaks there is no ignoring it."[82]

I remember a time God spoke clearly to me right when I needed it. Phil was traveling to far-off places, and once again, I was alone. Once again, I was losing a battle with fear.

Night was most often when fear became an unmanageable monster. After tucking the kids into bed, I'd walk through our home praying for protection. Our house backed up to a green space, beautiful and solitary. I loved that vista during the day. But as darkness fell, the scene outside my window turned threatening, leaving me feeling vulnerable, unprotected. Who would hear if someone smashed those basement windows? Who would guard us against intruders? How does a mother without hearing guard her children while they sleep? While *she* sleeps?

I had my prayers for protection all figured out. I prayed for angels, for guardians, for something I'd heard about in a sermon called a "hedge of protection." I prayed that God would stay awake so I could sleep soundly. But night after night, I tossed and turned, sleep deprivation making me crazy with anxiety.

One night, as I was praying all those worried petitions (as if God needed to be reminded over and over again to watch over us), I heard Him tell me to *stop*. It had been a long day of car-pooling rain-confined kids with too little sleep the night before. By the time I got the kids to bed, I was too tired to do anything but take a hot bath and hope for a better day tomorrow. As I soaked away the tension in my big bathtub under a circle of window, a full moon positioned itself right in the middle of my view. Instead of relishing its luminosity, I worried that a full moon purportedly brings out the crazy in people. Would this be the night someone slipped past the protection for which I prayed so diligently?

Suddenly I felt my Father's rebuke.

"Enough, Di! I don't want you to pray for protection anymore."

Clearly as if He was right there, I heard Him speak into my foolishness. Not a severe scolding; no shaming; it was more like a firm Father prying my trembling fingers from the control I felt I must maintain at all times. For long moments, in that big bathtub, I soaked in His message of care.

"Of course I'll watch over you. But you've got to trust Me. I came that you might have life, and this worry-filled tension is sucking the life right out of you."

Then, in the gentle but firm way He has often spoken to me, He reminded me of my own father, how every night without fail, Dad walked through our house checking doors, locking up, turning the heater down, setting things to rights. How I'd felt the safeness of his care. How I'd trusted my dad, never once begging him to lock the doors or keep the boogeyman out.

That night, I heard my heavenly Father tell me to stop pleading and start giving thanks to Him for all those nights of protection, for decades of security, for a life thus far free of the disasters I dreaded.

So I did. Never again did I wake up in fear—not once.

That nightly ritual of giving thanks worked like a powerful sleeping pill, putting my soul to rest in the hands of the only One who can keep me safe. I don't think a thousand sermons could have penetrated deep enough into my fear to put me in that place of peace. But just a few words from the Lord, heard in the silence of my broken ears, accomplished what I could not.

Over and over again in the Scriptures, God issues His short decree: *Fear not*. But it wasn't until I heard those words myself that His rebuke changed my reality.

A *rebuke* is a soft sweeping of His thoughts against mine, reminding me of what I already know.

I often hear His rebuke through Scripture, from a story that could have been written with my name on it. Like when Abraham caved to Sarah's fussing that maybe God needed help fulfilling His promise of a much-wanted son for the two of them. Her plan to "solve the problem" by forcing her maid into a surrogate pregnancy sent them into a season of unrest that continues to this day. The descendants of that venture have been warring with Abraham's other offspring for centuries since.[83]

Paul wrote, "These things happened to them as examples for us. They were written down to warn us . . . If you think you are standing strong, be careful not to fall."[84]

Strong words.

But even as I am pulled up short, remembering not to "do a Sarah," God leads me to another grace-filled passage where Sarah is celebrated for choosing to "do what is right without being frightened by any fear."[85]

God uses these stories, true and raw and vividly recorded, to warn me of the turmoil that lies ahead if I choose a faithless path. This One whose wisdom spans the centuries brings real stories into my life and shows me the way to rest. I read the stories and He speaks truth and wisdom and rightness, showing me "the right way to go." The way I should take lest I trip myself right into a miry, mucky pit[86] from which I'd undoubtedly mess up my own story.

When I say that God speaks in the silence, this is what I mean.

He speaks, using words that guide us in life and fill our minds with rest. "Here's the paradox: If we don't listen, we never enter His rest. Yet if we don't enter His rest, we never listen."[87]

Sometimes we just can't hear through the hollering of our own relentless worry. And so we wonder if God has gone silent, if He's awake when we need Him most.

One morning, I walked out early to retrieve the newspaper that had been tossed on the driveway. Barefoot, I ventured out in near-total silence—no hearing aids amplifying sounds that barely registered. As I wrapped my robe around me, the silence seemed to close in. I felt the weight of it, the way sounds fell flat, as if my breath could not expand in that deadness. Looking around, I knew noises were waking the world, but I couldn't hear them.

The garbage truck down the street, the car idling at the four-way stop. A child riding by on his bicycle without even a rattle to let me know he was there. All of a sudden, my whole world felt unsafe, foreign, with me trapped in a suffocating cell of sound-lessness. It felt as if the air had gone out of an invisible room all around me. My heart raced wildly as I panicked at the sense of claustrophobia that encompassed me in the silence.

Scurrying back into the house as fast as I could, breathless and shaken, I slammed the door behind me as if to shut out the sound of that silence. It took a while for my breathing to calm, and when it did, I opened my Bible to the spot I'd prepared for that morning's listening. I needed to hear from God.

It was a well-worn place He'd led me to often in Psalms: "Be still, and know that I am God."[88]

I breathed Him in, great draughts of life-giving assurance that I was safe, that He was bigger than the silence, that He could hear what I could not, and I could trust Him to care for me.

Turning to the New Testament to drink in Jesus' words, I found another favorite: "Come to Me, all who are weary and heavy-laden, and I will give you rest. Take My yoke upon you, and learn from Me, for I am gentle and humble in heart; and you will find rest for your souls. For My yoke is easy and My burden is light."[89]

Yes! Rest, He seemed to say, must be chosen.

The choosing of rest is a decision not to worry or fret or fuss furiously on some bone of circumstantial contention. When I choose rest, I purposely obey my Master, dropping that gnawed bit of problem at His feet, leaving it for Him to figure out while I trot happily at the end of His lead. He will not yank me into rest; instead, He invites me to sit beside Him in the quiet stillness of His lordship.[90]

Choose rest, Di.

Is that just me talking to myself? Maybe. But I'm not nearly as nice to myself as He is. All too often, I lambast myself for being dense, for not doing better, for slipping into fretting. He doesn't do that.

I can lay hold of the calm I so badly need by listening to the Spirit, who uses His Word to reprove and rebuke and remind and exhort me. In order to enter that rest, I must choose.

The same is true for all of us. I have come to believe that, just like me, *anyone who is willing* can learn to recognize His voice and wonder at a God who invites us to hear.

He wants each of us to know that He means it when He says, "Come to me with your ears wide open. Listen, and you will find life."[91]

CHAPTER 8

Alluring Me to Listen . . .

a story about intimacy

Several years after my initial diagnosis, our family of six moved from California to Oregon. We'd lived there while Phil was going to grad school, and I looked forward to living in the Pacific Northwest again, with all its lush beauty. Phil had accepted a position as a worship pastor at a church on the west side of Portland, and our kids jumped right into new friends and new adventures.

It was harder for me. By then, I was wearing the biggest hearing aids available, cranked on high. If anyone tried to hug me, those giant amplifiers squealed in protest, startling whoever got that close. Explaining over and over that I wore hearing aids and telling people not to worry only resulted in more confusion. I'd tell my story and try to make everyone feel okay, but how do you insert into an awkwardly one-way conversation the caveat, "by-the-way-I'm-going-deaf-so-please-talk-louder"?

Phil, who pulled me close through every step of my convoluted journey, tried hard to include me in every conversation. The idea of leaving me out in order to make it easier on others never occurred to him.

Whenever I stepped back, distancing myself from another dialogue that would make no sense to me, Phil insisted on playing the role of play-by-play commentator. To my chagrin, he'd pause a conversation long enough to insist that I look in his face while he summarized what was being said in the distinct talking-to-a-deaf-person-dialect that he knew I'd be most likely to understand. If my eyes registered the blank incomprehension that marked so many of our conversations, he'd lean in closer, change the words, simplify what he was saying.

My body grew hot with embarrassment with all those eyes staring at the spectacle of a deafened woman craning to hear. I wanted to run and hide. But there stood my husband, unwilling to let me cower in a corner alone, his grin making the oddity of our performance in front of an abashed audience seem less like a circus and more like *normal*.

To my husband, this new normal *was* normal. He adapted himself to my hearing loss like it was the most natural thing in the world.

Still, other people's embarrassment fueled my own. I wanted to talk about ordinary things like soccer practice and where to get my hair cut. What I didn't want was to be branded as that woman who was *different*.

That woman who was *deaf*.

To my dismay, one woman I tried to befriend at our new church turned a cold shoulder my way, telling another new friend that she thought I was odd. Apparently, I'd failed to hear her talking and blurted something benign right over her story.

How many times were faux pas like this happening without me realizing it? Mistakes like these drove me further into a shell of silence. I watched, but said very little.

I came to dread the drive-thru. I'd roll down my window, letting in the roar of nearby traffic, then shush my chattering children in the backseat and strain to make sense of sounds that made no sense. After a half dozen repetitions of "What? What'd you say? Can you repeat that please?" I'd give up in embarrassment and just wait for my turn at the window, where I mostly blundered my way through an order. I wanted to scream at the kid in the apron to *slow down! Look at me! Talk slow and clear, and give me a chance!*

Instead, I smiled and pretended to be like every other flustered mom with a van full of kids.

Carpooling my son to the high school across town was exhausting. I couldn't hear what anybody said from the backseat and didn't dare ask questions when I knew I wouldn't hear the answers. So I simply smiled and acted as if I hadn't a care in the world, all the while wishing I could know my son's friends, wishing the wall of silence separating me from everyday small talk could somehow be breached. I knew it embarrassed him, noticed how he didn't look at me while we were driving, how he diverted the conversation to topics meant for just his buddies. When I asked him about it once, he just shrugged his shoulders in that accepting way kids have and said, "It's okay, mom. You can't help it."

But it wasn't okay; not with me.

By the time my youngest was ten, he was making most of my phone calls for me. With the other kids busy with high school, it was up to Matt to be my ears. I'd coach him on what to say, what questions to expect, what I needed to know. He'd clear his throat, purposely lowering his voice to sound older than he was.

Haircuts, doctor's visits, RSVPs—he made himself sound like a personal assistant to a professional rather than the buzz-cut kid he really was.

When the kids were young, it seemed like the most normal thing in the world to have a mother who couldn't hear. They adapted, made do, easily accepting my disability with the grace unique to children.

Until they entered their teen years.

By the time my oldest daughter, Rebekah, was in high school, I could hardly hear at all.

Making sense of sounds was becoming arduously hard work. Much of the time, no matter how slavishly I tried, I couldn't make out what I was supposed to hear.

Rebekah remembers those years as a conflicting seesaw between her feelings of loyalty to me, her mom, and acute embarrassment at my disability. She'd cringe when I talked too loud because I couldn't hear myself over ambient noise and instinctively spoke louder.

The inability to modulate the volume of my own voice still plagues me. I have to consciously think about what the appropriate volume feels like as I use my voice. The rumble of my vocal cords, is it too rough? Am I too loud? Too soft?

I missed names when Rebekah's friends came over, not once or twice, but repeatedly. It's hard to remember the difference between Cara and Tara when you can't hear the *c* or the *t*. Soft consonants barely registered. After a while, I learned to stay on the outskirts of my daughter's social life rather than attempt to engage an already self-conscious adolescent.

But I didn't like it. I didn't want to keep my distance from my daughter's friends.

Rebekah remembers the frustration of having to touch me to get my attention, to wait until I turned toward her when she needed to speak to me. Often, I'd throw out a question and fail to turn from my task to "see" her answer. She grew weary of repeating things over and over and then hated herself for being irritated. She would vacillate back and forth between frustration with me and irritation at other people for not doing a better job of accommodating my disability.

Her "typical" teenage years bore the burden of all that conflict badly. I sensed her moodiness but couldn't find a way in. Our relationship suffered wild swings between the intimacy of two people whose differences made us like each other all the more, and incongruent moments of unspoken frustration.

How could she talk to me about what she didn't understand herself?

When I had so little hearing left, the only way I could be sure to hear was if I found a quiet corner and concentrated intently on the words of the one I wanted to hear. My kids knew to beckon me to that place of silence in order to talk. Even my friends—those who were willing to do the hard work of being a friend to an introverted deaf woman—knew to meet me in a quiet place in order to be heard.

Phil had it down to a science.

I married an extreme extrovert. Phil thinks out loud, forming opinions and solidifying thoughts as his mouth moves. When he has a decision to make, he uses me as his sounding board, approaching the problem from all angles, discussing, asking for input, weighing options.

Ironically, his biggest need from me is to listen. To nod and affirm, to question and probe. He wants my opinion, my thoughts, my take on the matter at hand.

During my going-deaf years, he learned to lead me into a place far away from noise so we could talk. When we lived in Santa Cruz, we'd sit on the back deck. Something about the stillness of outside makes hearing much easier.

After we moved to Oregon and the rain chased us inside, he made sure to make space in our room for a quiet retreat. He'd build a fire, brew us some coffee, shoo the kids out the door, and talk to me. How much easier it would have been for him to just leave me alone, to forgo all that trouble and let me live in the disconnected world of the hard of hearing. But he wouldn't. Instead, he persistently pursued time to talk with me.

It was my husband's persistence that opened my heart to see that God does the same.

In fact, this aloneness with us is so important to Him that He tells us a story, part real life tragedy and part metaphor, in order to paint a picture of His longing to be close.

It's the story of Hosea, and it starts with these words: "The word of the LORD that came to Hosea . . ."[92]

Right away, it seems, He lets us know that He speaks. The story goes on to tell how God asks Hosea to marry Gomer, a "promiscuous woman," a prostitute.[93] He wants their love to be a vivid picture of God's relentless pursuit of His people.

They have a family together: two sons and a daughter, each named to indicate something significant about God's care for His people.[94] But after a time, Gomer strays. She runs away from this one who loves her with fierce devotion, into the arms of others who bear gifts of fine clothes, "wool and linen," and fancy dinners.[95]

How can God use a broken relationship to show the world the wholeness of His love? The same way He wants to use our hard-of-hearing tendencies to bring us close and to speak the words we need to hear.

"Therefore I am now going to allure her; I will lead her into the wilderness and speak tenderly to her."[96]

Underlined and highlighted and starred in my Bible are these words: "So let us know, let us press on to know the LORD . . ."[97]

God's love for us is so inured to our deaf ears, so relentlessly determined to win us, so intent on intimacy that He invites us in to hear the throbbing of His heart. I can hardly grasp that kind of love. In my early mornings tucked into the silence, He allures me through His Word. To paraphrase the Amplified Bible, "I will speak tenderly *and* to her heart."[98]

My heart opens wide as I sip tea and listen. I hear tender words of correction. I hear wise words about how to live well. I fill journals with what I know He is saying, direction about who needs what and what He wants from me.

More than anything else, I hear tenderness. That He likes me just as I am. That He loves me too much to leave me just as I have always been. I hear His wanting to be with me, alone and still. I hear quiet. I hear rest. I breathe Him in and listen.

And He uses other means to talk to me as well—His Creation, for one. "For since the creation of the world God's invisible qualities—his eternal power and divine nature—have been clearly seen, being understood from what has been made . . ."[99]

Albert Einstein was known to have said, "Never lose a holy curiosity." And so I take my holy curiosity on my walks, intent to hear, watching for what the Creator is saying.

On one of my walks, when I needed a chance to blow off steam about a constantly chaotic house in the stream of too much company, He spoke to me about my incessant need for order. As if He had joined me on my foray in the woods, I sensed Him pointing to His created world. I saw His ease with messiness, that the kind of beauty He creates is not golf-course perfect. Twigs and leaves and weeds and wildflowers wither messily into an insulating mulch, which in turn feeds trees and causes ferns to flourish.

How could I help but hear? My need was not so much for every towel to be hung just so, or for the sink to shine empty, but to fling open my home for that season, inviting beauty to flourish in the people who came in for shelter.

He also uses circumstances to speak to me, but I've learned to tread with caution there. We once had a sincere friend who claimed God had told him to start a lighting store because he had read, "I am the Light of the world."[100] When his business failed, plunging him into bankruptcy, he couldn't understand what went wrong.

The problem with circumstances is that we assume God wants everything to turn out hunky-dory for us. Your house sells quickly, so you're sure He's leading in the move. You're offered a scholarship to a college far away, so you're certain this is His way of "opening doors."

Maybe, but maybe not. Like reading tea leaves, circumstances shift and change too easily to assign God's will to their every movement.

Of the myriad ways I hear God speak, it has been through listening in community—specifically through the friendships of women—that He has taught me the most about who I am. But learning from friends came slow and hard for me, a side-trip in my story that caused me to initially shun the very friendships I needed.

Of all of the difficulties I encountered during my slide into deafness, it was my "communication disorder's"[101] impairment to friendship that molded me the most. I always had friends, plenty of friends. Growing up in the expat community centered around

Frankfurt International School, my friends were my tribe in the midst of a foreign land. British, Israeli, American, and German, these were friendships based not on cultural commonality, but grounded in the close-knit community of families away from home. Friendships there came easily, everyone purposefully cultivating the same soil in which to flourish. We needed each other, and since there were so few of us, we couldn't be picky about whom we befriended.

Then we came home to the U.S., and a church full of friends reached out to me and brought me with them into a faith I would have never embraced but for their insistence on caring for me.

Though introverted by nature and shy in social situations, with my girlfriends I could be my less-than-graceful self. I could laugh and be teased and worry out loud about all the things that worry women.

Marrying a man who was a pastor shifted that easy camaraderie. I learned early as I stepped into that foreign territory that I had to be extra guarded—*discerning*, as I called it—lest someone get too close and poke holes in the image I believed I needed to present.

To my surprise, people in our congregation sometimes invaded our world as if they owned us. They made suggestions as to how we could do better, commented on how tired, thin, stressed, or fashionable I looked. Old friends were quick to criticize changes that new friends felt imperative to point out needed changing. Those pricks of criticism hurt every time, but it was the dawning realization that some people felt it was their duty to "confront me in love" that caused me to withdraw into a very tight, very small circle of friends.

Being part of a large church compounded the unease I felt as my worship leader husband was exalted to superstar status. He was tall and handsome, with a winning smile and a way with words that seemed to usher our whole church right into the presence of the One we were worshiping. I played my part by wearing beautiful dresses in all the best-for-me colors, poofing my '80s bangs up big, and always, always looking my painted-on best. I had no understanding of the barrier that kind of polished beauty can erect between women. No inkling that by pretending to be perfect, I was setting myself up for all that poking so common to the gender of Eve.

As children came along and dresses and heels segued into jogging suits and running shoes, I breathed a little more easily. We were all in this together, swapping ideas and survival techniques about sleepless nights, nursing babies, and defiant toddlers. Once again, I'd found a tribe, this time of young moms, whose language was my own. Trying to be perfect with a red-faced toddler threatening to bring my world down around his will became laughable. I was one of them, and we carried the burden of the motherhood season together.

When my hearing started to become muffled and listening took more work, I was unprepared for how it would impact my relationships.

One woman in particular stunned me with her seeming inability to cope with my difficulty hearing. She was one of those gentle women whose speech was as soft as her personality. We'd swapped horror stories of our boys' antics, laughing in that particular way of mothers in the trenches. I liked her, valued our friendship. When I finally got desperate enough to break through my embarrassment and ask her to speak louder, she just couldn't. Couldn't even try. Something inside of her shrank from my disability, resisting any urging to increase the volume of her speech. I wanted to hear, wanted to hear *her*, but no amount of asking helped. When I mentioned my struggles or fiddled with my hearing aids to get the squealing to stop, she shuddered and looked away, as if seeing the slightest glimpse of my suffering hurt her too much to come close.

All I saw was her rejection of *me,* and that rejection stung deep.

Other friends politely pretended that nothing was wrong.

My world was falling apart, but they couldn't cross the social boundary that might make them seem insensitive to my disability. We'd all been taught by our '50s-era parents not to stare at the man in the wheelchair. Now, many of my friends saw my hearing aids in the same light. I wanted to talk about it, needed them to see me in my struggles, to bend into my space just far enough to let me know they saw and cared. Instead, they pretended not to notice, and I played into their discomfort by making myself disappear.

Over time, I withdrew into the safety of a very small group. My husband, my parents and my in-laws, a few friends. I learned to avoid talking to people I felt certain I wouldn't understand. It felt safer not to be rejected, and I learned to live with the loneliness.

Sunday became a dreaded day. By the time I got home from church with hungry kids and a tired husband, my shoulders ached with bunched up muscles from straining to catch every last drop of conversation. The aches got so bad I went to my doctor to see what was wrong. When tests came back with no real cause, she concluded that the stress of trying to hear was wearing me out.

I decided I didn't need friends, didn't need to process out loud the turmoil on my insides. I had my husband, my children, the ever-shrinking circle of people I allowed to remain close. What's more, I thought I didn't have room for friends. With four children, two dogs, two cats, and two horses, who has the luxury of going out with girlfriends? If I wasn't cleaning, combing, washing, doctoring, cooking, or serving somewhere, I was curled up with a book. Books became my safe place, a retreat from ministry to feed my mind and soothe my soul.

Friends just seemed like more responsibility. One more person to figure out how to hear, one more woman who wanted to talk on the phone, one more afternoon of exhausting listening.

But I was wrong about not needing friends—so very wrong. I was so far out in the left field of denial, in fact, it's a wonder that my few friends stuck it out at all.

When my husband and oldest son started a church together ten years ago, a group of passionate, newly-Jesus-following young women swept me into their hearts and would not let me go. They determined to adopt me as their "mom," and spilled their hurts and struggles all over me, confiding in me their unedited stories of abuse and abandonment.

The darkness that haunted them from their forays into sexual promiscuity and addiction unshackled me from the self-inflicted chains that had cut me off from friendship. If they could be so raw, couldn't I?

When, tentatively, I shared with them my own rebellion, these girls fairly glued their hearts to mine. I was one of them! As I grew bolder and allowed them deeper into what one friend termed my "cave," they began to listen to me, not as the mentor I'd tried to be, but as a woman desperate to hear God.

God began to bring other women—my age, imperfect, and bent at strange angles, but beautiful in their honest humanness. How I have laughed with these friends! They pull me out of myself into the broad adventure of relationship. We went to Haiti together, a whole group of us, women in their twenties to their fifties, and there we connected with women from another world. I'd been invited to teach a group of pastors' wives, and I asked if I could bring my friends with me. Together we taught, and together we learned. When makeup ran down our faces in the intense heat and humidity, we went gloriously naked from all those face coverings that cost so much time and money. I couldn't remember a time I had gone public just-as-I-am. My friends did my hair up in ponytails and laughed as I learned to dance in my stiff white-church-lady way, to the delight of our Haitian sisters.

Every one of them poured love on every one of us: leaders in our churches, teachers, mothers, many of us married to preachers. No language could separate us because we saw each other's joys and sorrows. Those women welcomed us into what A. W. Tozer termed the "fellowship of the burning hearts."[102]

When we got home, six of the women who had gone on the trip banded together to become "The Sistas." Though I have remained connected with all of the women I traveled with, these few give me something in community I have never had before. They are my spiritual peers. By this, I mean that for the first time in a long, long time, I have women in my life who do not need me to teach them or lead them or be an example to them.

They teach *me*. They lead *me*. They chart a course for me to follow as they machete their own paths through the jungles of all those voracious feelings that tangle women into messes.

And not one of them hesitates to talk LOUD to me. They've gotten over the politeness that once separated us, and have insisted that I do, too. I don't have to be careful with my Sistas, though they'd be the first to let me know in no uncertain terms if I got off track.

These women know me as the broken, mixed-up mess that is the real me. And they still like me! They ask me to pray, they text at crazy hours, often waking me up to needs that only The Sistas know because only The Sistas can be trusted to talk to no one but the Father about the needs. Because of this, they have brought me closer to my Father, whose acceptance of me *just-as-I-am-right-now-in-this-less-than-holy-moment* astounds me every day.

I have learned, by stumbling and tripping and jerking my way down this uneven path toward community, that withdrawing from friendships stunted my walk with God, limiting my understanding of who He is and how He loves.

It didn't have to happen.

All those years of unacknowledged loneliness were a result of my own self-protectiveness and pride. I wanted to be liked more than I wanted to be honest, to be thought well of rather than embraced for who I really was. And so I let a few ill-equipped people be my excuse for not engaging in the hard work of raw, honest friendship.

I regret it now.

I see it for what it is and fight hard to keep myself from slipping back into that place of too much independence and isolation.

There is a story told by Matthew[103] and by Mark[104] and again by Luke[105] about a man with four determined friends. These men carried their paralyzed friend to Jesus, and encountering formidable obstacles, dug through the dirt and debris to do whatever it took to get their friend to His feet. There is no indication that the poor man was directing them or insisting on their help. His healing happened not because of his faith alone, but because of the faith of his friends: "When Jesus saw *their* faith, he said to the man, 'Take heart, son; your sins are forgiven . . . Get up, take your mat and go home.'"[106]

I love this story, even though it goes against my natural bent toward introverted seclusion. Had it been me, my friends would have had to reach deep into my cave and pull me out!

There are times in our lives, *hard-of-hearing* times, when the pain of our suffering drowns out any chance to hear God for ourselves. Wrapped in our own paralysis, we lie passively wishing, not daring to believe that God is good or that He hears or cares. That is when the risks we took in working hard at Spirit-centered community will make all the difference in our ability to hear God. Our friends will listen *for* us, and often, without our direction or consent, will bring us to the feet of Jesus, full of their own unwavering faith.

There is another facet I love about this story, one I've repeated over and over to myself in my own story. When Jesus spoke, it was not to the man's friends, but to the man directly. He gave him something to do, something hard, something seemingly impossible.

Get up. Take your mat. Go home.

He didn't call his friends to gather 'round and help, to pick him up and assist with those first fumbling steps. He just spoke clearly and waited for the man to obey. Or not. And because he did, "the crowd saw this, they were filled with awe; and they praised God . . ."[107]

That is what listening in community is about.

In our weakness, our friends who love Jesus and believe in His love for us catch us up and carry us to His feet. In that place, surrounded by those witnesses, we are faced with our own choice to listen and obey. Or not. But often, the care and compassion of friends leads us out of our self-pity and compels us to take constructive action.

Now I understand how much I need His people—not for self-validation, but for spiritual survival.

When I am weak is when I need them the most. I need real relationships with people who are following hard after Jesus and recognizing their own brokenness and need for redemption.

I need people who will allow me to fail but won't allow me to fall too far.

I need women in my life who know that I'm not "good" and love me still, because they see that I'm being redeemed by the One who is.

While I need honest friends who help me to hear Him, it is still up to me to position myself to listen, because wearing hearing aids changes the way I hear. Instead of sound coming to me in a natural and easy way, the way it floats into the wide-open ears of most people, I have to intentionally go after those sounds, figure them out, and interpret them.

In the audiologist's chamber, I learned that in order to hear, I had to hold still. All outside sounds were sealed out, but my inner self could be just noisy enough to cause me to miss what I wanted to hear. In that heavy silence every movement from me was magnified—rubbing my nose, shifting in my seat, fiddling with the button on my blouse. It all interfered with hearing those beeps or distinguishing those barely perceptible differences that make it possible to understand. To get it right.

I also learned early on that if I wanted to hear someone talking, I had to position myself a certain way or else I'd end up inadvertently eavesdropping on a conversation behind me and understanding very little of what the person speaking to me was saying.

In restaurants, that means tucking myself into a corner with a wall behind me and facing the speaker. I have to steer clear of the clatter from the kitchen or the roar of the coffee grinder. Outside usually works best because sounds don't ricochet off walls and ceilings, but if there are cars whizzing by or fountains splashing or pedestrians walking and talking and throwing out noise, forget it.

I have to adapt. To pay attention and concentrate and think through the best way to hear.

It's not so different from learning to listen to God.

I have come to see how important it is to know the way our own "hearing" works. When we try to copy someone else or follow certain instructions because that's the way everyone else does it, we might miss out on the unique messages He has just for us.

I am not like my friend Penny, who hears in pictures and metaphors and dreams and mystical signs. Nor am I like my daughter, Rebekah, whose intelligent logic makes perfect sense to her but sounds too smart for me, as if she's hearing answers to questions I haven't thought to ask and thrills in purest worship over statistical evidence that leaves me bewildered. I am not like my husband, who hears in straightforward facts and listens as a loyal servant waiting for orders, waiting to hear what God wants, searching for wisdom to help him do life in a way that pleases the Lord.

Me, I hear words. Beautiful words woven artfully to capture the heart of an idea. This is why I keep a stack of different translations of the Bible within easy reach. Even the way words are placed on a page can help me hear more clearly. *What is He saying? What does He mean by that word? What does He want me to know?*

And I hear best alone. Curled up in a quiet corner by a window or sitting out on the back deck of my parents' cabin in the mountains with all creation glistening in the sunshine, I hear so clearly it's as if He's right there next to me.

Sometimes, at home, I'll sit outside under a tiny overhang while the Oregon rain washes my world clean. Breathing in His creation, I hear things I'd never catch in a coffee shop or surrounded by windowless walls.

I think that's what God means when He urges His listeners to "Be still, and know that I am God."[108] The Hebrew word for "still" means to "let drop, to abandon, to let alone, to refrain." And that's how we hear His whispers. By stilling ourselves, abandoning all those worries for a while, quieting those voices in our heads.

Shhh.

First, we have to recognize how noisy we are. That we scold ourselves, push ourselves, argue with the person in our head. It took me years to figure this out. This person (who is me) sits on my shoulder whispering meanness in my ear. Sometimes a demon or two joins in the refrain. *You're not enough, you should, you shouldn't have, you ought to, shame on you.* And *shame on him, he shouldn't have, why did he?* On and on we go with that noisy diatribe. No wonder we can't hear God's love! No wonder we're uptight and defensive and prickly around others.

Second, we have to make a conscious choice. After recognizing all of our not-so-nice self-talk, it's up to us to choose to silence it. To turn it off. And we have to make that choice over and over again. More than once, I've gone out on a walk intending to refresh myself and listen to God, only to find that I'm duking it out with the person in my head. I take hold of those ravings and center myself on God—for about fifty strides. Too soon, though, I find myself slipping back into the same pattern, fighting feelings I've repeatedly confessed as sin. But over time, with the firm conviction that self-stillness is the route to hearing God, I have become quicker to rebound.

One path to stillness is to sit without distractions, hands open in a symbolic stance of receiving. *I am here to hear. To hear You.* Mentally and emotionally and spiritually and physically sitting or kneeling in silent expectation that He is speaking, and believing that although we may hear nothing at the moment, it is just a matter of time until we do.

In order to hear God accurately, we need to turn off all the clamoring sounds around us. The ding of the computer that announces the arrival of an email. The insistent ring of the phone and the vibration of incoming messages. The buzzers and reminders and alarms that inundate our lives with urgency. We have to turn them off, to set aside a good amount of time for silence. Space to just listen to God. To wait for Him.

To be still enough to hear.

It is easier for me in one respect, I think. My deafness allows me a luxury few others can indulge in. Waking up in the morning without my listening devices, I cannot hear any outside noises. Nothing. No rings or whistles, no children crying, not so much as a truck rumbling by. My world is as silent as that sound booth.

Still, just like someone who hears, I have to turn it all off. To turn aside from my relentless inner monologue and listen close. To be still and know that He is God and to relish His words to me. To wait in quiet expectation for what He has to say.

When I do, He meets me there. He adjusts the volume of His voice for me, alluring me to listen.

He speaks in my silence.

CHAPTER 9

The Sound of Rain . . .

a story of His presence

It *was my year* to host Thanksgiving. I'd looked forward to this day for months: planning, researching recipes, thinking through everyone's favorites, combining all the traditional dishes we'd grown to love with new ideas I was sure would please the palates of my children, now grown.

From the east, a frigid wind blew through the gorge with ferocious strength, its tail whipping the mighty Columbia River into whitecaps, unleashing icy rain and creating treacherous conditions. I watched in wonder from my kitchen window, safe and warm. I was excited by the prospect of the day, hoping the electricity could withstand the storm long enough for me to get dinner on the table.

The table glistened with old silver and fragile crystal my mother had collected during our years in Germany. My grandma's old blue willow china added richness while a hodge-podge of serving dishes contributed just the right element of charm. As my family arrived, coming in from the storm, shedding coats and embracing each other, my heart swelled. After all the years of creating opportunities for friendship, sometimes forcing them to get along, even demanding they make apologies to each other when intervention was necessary, years when I truly doubted that this strong-willed bunch would ever all agree—now, they'd grown into real friends.

Phil and I looked at each other, and I knew just what he was thinking: all the hard years of parenting were worth it for this, this circle of family. I breathed it in, the safety of my tribe. While outside the storm raged, here at our hearth the warmth of their comradeship roared and crackled and filled me to bursting with the joy of it.

This was the kind of day I had dreamed about when the chaos of our rambunctious family drove me to distraction. In those days, when the bathroom was my place of refuge, when I could barely keep my head above the mounds of laundry and ever-emptying fridge, I'd comforted myself with Norman Rockwell-like imaginings of our crew all grown up. And here it was, in real life, these people I loved, laughing and teasing and loving and debating and talking on top of one another.

Our family is full of communicators with a capital C, and I can't help but find that more than a little bit laughable. How did a progressively deafening mother manage to raise a bunch of avid talkers?

I sat right in the middle, where I would be surrounded by conversation, able to see each dear face. I'd made sure my powerful hearing aids had fresh batteries, adjusted the settings for optimal control. I was ready.

When they finally quieted, we held hands and spilled our thanks to the One who had been redeeming and growing this family into a people of grace. While everyone else bowed, I kept my head up and my eyes open, reading Phil's lips as he prayed, lest I miss one precious word.

With Phil's *Amen!* came more noise, more talking, more laughing and slapping the table and more debate about what, who, and why, and all the inside jokes that no one else could have possibly figured out.

And I, who should have been drinking it in, relishing the results of so many years of hoping, sat silent.

I couldn't understand a word.

The conversation swirled and laughter swelled, sound echoing off the walls, bouncing erratically, blocking out my limited ability to grasp and hold on to any clarity. All I could hear was a cacophony of unidentifiable noise.

I sank inside myself. Why hadn't I thought of this possibility? The quiet of our now empty nest had lulled me into forgetting the noise a family of six can generate. All those voices!

Those old feelings of abandonment and isolation rushed back. All those years, all that work, all my anticipation of what would finally be, and here I sat, encased in my silent world, set apart from everyone I loved, unable to make sense of anything they said.

I tried to focus on just one face, straining to understand. Nothing. Laughter rang out in a shared moment of hilarity. I looked from face to face. *I have no idea what they're saying. This is worse than I ever could have imagined. If I'd known how hard deafness would be all those years ago when the doctors first told me it was inevitable, I would have despaired. I am alone in a room full of my favorite people. So alone.*

There was nothing anyone could do to stop the downward spiral, but my audiologist still needed to see me annually. Even though there was no hope of improvement, tracking those beeps and whistles onto a chart to reveal the deterioration of my hearing seemed to be the official course. It had now been nearly twenty years since that initial diagnosis, by now my test results were nearing the bottom of the hearing graph.

I continued to dread those tests. Something inside me still needed to prove something—that I was competent, that my lack of hearing didn't define me, that I could beat the test. Every year, I'd leave with my evaluation in hand, the words "slight subjective loss" letting me know that there couldn't be too many more years before there were no more sounds to lose.

It was time for my annual evaluation, and I couldn't help but dread what I knew was coming. As my car wound up the road to "Pill Hill," the vast complex of medical offices and hospitals and research facilities that hovers above Portland, I gripped the steering wheel with clammy hands, talking myself out of a sickening sense of doom. I was fairly certain I'd lost more ground, that what little residual hearing was left wasn't much use. *This is it*, I thought. What I'd hoped would never happen would most certainly be confirmed today.

I had a different audiologist, having long since moved from Santa Cruz. Like Janna before her, Allison had become my mentor, my teacher, my guide. Leading me once again into the soundproof chamber, she tested me with all the beeps and whistles and phrases I had become so familiar with. As usual, I felt a completely irrational sense of failure when for long stretches I heard nothing. A few faint buzzes, times when the silence seemed "busy," but not much else.

When Allison went through the usual list of words, asking me to repeat them, I knew I was only guessing my way through. I couldn't hear, couldn't understand, couldn't rummage up any hope that maybe I'd escape with no more loss.

I experienced a sense of déjà vu when Allison, just like Janna, climbed down from her control room full of computers and knobs and recordings, drew up a cold metal chair, and sat with my chart in her lap. We looked at each other with no words to fill the silence.

I knew what she would say, could have said it for her.

"Diane, your loss has now entered the category we consider profound. You missed so much that I'm amazed you can understand me at all. Even with hearing aids on, you could barely understand the sentences. I can see that you are functionally deaf—there just isn't enough hearing left—I'm sorry. "

My "baby," Elizabeth—the one I had begged God to allow me to hear—had just turned eighteen, a full-fledged woman. Rebekah, our joy-filled middle daughter, had finally found her beautiful adult self after years of complex, intelligent, creative, people-loving quandaries. John Mark, the son who has always asked more questions than any mama could answer, was full steam into seminary, with a calling on his life to get the answers and rephrase them for a generation desperate to know. And

Matthew, the one I'd worried wouldn't learn to talk, was chattering his way happily through middle school.

By God's inexplicable grace, my family was thriving, each one following Him, all determined to stay connected to their mom who couldn't hear.

Still, that mother's need to listen drove me to want more than reading lips and jotting notes. I longed to interact more with my children—to hear their secrets, to call them on the phone, to joke and tease and hear their laughter.

During the past several years, I'd started hearing more and more talk of a newly developing medical device called a cochlear implant. Hailed as a medical miracle, some claimed it would banish deafness forever. No more babies born to live the rest of their lives encased in silence. By implanting a computer into their heads in those first critical years, while their brains could still develop neural pathways with which to process speech, deafness could become a thing of the past.

I was skeptical at first. A computer in my head? It sounded like just another hearing aid, albeit fancier and far more expensive. But I couldn't resist checking out the online discussion boards filled with people who were seriously considering such a drastic move. I listened in, prowling about the perimeters, never adding to the discussion, just absorbing information.

What I sensed in those forums was a whole lot of angst. These were primarily people born deaf. People who had overcome so much adversity, finding community and sympathy in their tight circles of mostly deaf friends. They were asking each other questions I'd never considered, questions with no real right answer:

Should they alter the way they'd seemed destined to live? Would the new technology abolish deaf culture altogether? Was this a handicap or simply a difference?

It is a controversial decision, one fraught with political and cultural opposition. Banish deafness? The idea appalled many of the contributors to the forums. A child born deaf these days need not stay deaf. But many adults in the deaf culture believe that their deafness is part of their identity. And for parents to strip a child of his deafness and force hearing on him is likened by some to child abuse. Many deaf parents balk at the idea of implanting their deaf baby with a device that would surely bump their child out of the familiar confines of deaf culture. And for those who have been deaf all their lives, a cochlear implant would not give them the understanding they needed in order to process speech effectively. They would hear sounds, a huge help in itself, but unless that eighth bundle of nerves that enables the brain to interpret sounds is activated before the age of four, there is little chance for the neural pathways to develop enough to understand speech.

I searched in vain to find someone like me, deafened in early adulthood. There were plenty of people who were born deaf, yes. People whose deafness was brought on by aging, lots of those. But what about those of us (surely there must be more?) who were able to hear for most of their lives and can't bear the idea of losing their place in the world of verbal communication?

I had what the audiologists called "auditory memory." I knew what sounds should sound like. But still, so much of my potential to hear hinged on lining up the implant exactly along the tight twists of my cochlear nerve. When I asked Tak Katsumoto, my hearing aid specialist in California, what he thought, he cautioned me like a mother hen, telling me everything that could go wrong. He'd heard horror stories: bungled surgeries, facial nerves irreparably severed, balance affected. Tak had a story for every possibility. He showed me a picture of a woman whose sagging face broadcast all the nightmares I could imagine. Add to that the picture in my mind of a surgeon drilling through my skull, the scarring and stitches and the fear of pain.

I backed off for a while after that, sure that the risks far outweighed any potential advantages. Yet I couldn't quell the rising excitement that *maybe* it could work.

During the weeks when I was worrying and praying and chewing on the seemingly unsafe idea of undergoing surgery for an implant, one word kept popping up in every sermon I sat through: courage.

Every week, as I sat in the front row of our church, listening to Phil preach, that word grabbed my attention. I read his lips, often reading Phil's notes the night before, focused on understanding.

Fear not. Trust.

Phil didn't have any idea that I was wrestling with fear again, a new kind of fear. *I* didn't even understand that fear was what was keeping me from going forward. I thought I'd closed the door because of good, reliable research. I'd sought counsel and been warned against considering a cochlear implant.

So why did my heart catch at this word, courage? What was this insistence that I probe deeper, that I recognize my hesitancy for what it was—not caution based on facts, but fear based on what-ifs?

And why wouldn't that preacher-husband of mine stop harping about faith and trust and courage?

It took a long time for me to gather up the nerve to take the next step. Slowly, I began to sense God's hand at my back, gently guiding me to a place of courageous trust. Gradually, I began introducing Phil to my turmoil, knowing that he'd need to be fully on board if I were to undergo what seemed like such a drastic step. To my surprise, I discovered he'd been thinking about it too, giving me room to ruminate on my own lest he push me into a decision only I could make.

Together, we sought to learn more. We reviewed reams of information gleaned from the Internet, sent for reports from the manufacturers of the processors, read everything we could find about the surgery itself. The House Ear Institute in Los Angeles had pioneered the initial implants, so we wondered if we'd need to go south to learn more. Then we heard about a surgeon in Portland who was heralded as one of the best in his field. After months of referrals and pre-tests and more audiological exams, Dr. McMenomey ushered us into his office to discuss the possibility of a cochlear implant. He told us he'd never hit a facial nerve yet. Still, it sounded to me like he'd be relying on a lot of luck.

While Phil seemed as excited as a guy talking car engines, I was gulping nervously. Since any family story was bound to end up in a sermon, this one was no exception. That Sunday, Phil described to our congregation in gory detail how the surgeon would peel back my skull (it was actually only the skin) to stick a probe inside my brain (actually, in the cochlear nerve behind my ear, a long way from my brain). I cringed as he spoke. My friends looked appalled until I assured everyone that the surgery was relatively minor and nothing like the brain surgery intimated by my husband's story.

Dr. McMenomey ordered another round of tests, this time specifically to determine whether or not I met cochlear implant qualifications. Allison explained that in order to qualify for the surgery, I'd have to demonstrate an almost complete inability to understand and interpret the faint sound my ears could process. She would play her recording of sentences and individual words, and I would listen with my hearing aids on, repeating back exactly what I heard.

Since I'd become an expert at this test, I already knew the sentences, had figured out the whole procedure. Subject, verb, predicate. Simple sentences that made sense. I even knew which words would be used. *Cowboy, airplane, Indian, sidewalk, toothpaste.*

Sure enough, the recording I'd practically memorized from years and years of annual tests came through those speakers ever so faintly, without change or update.

In the sound booth, I leaned forward, quieted my breathing, and worked hard to get it, just as I had done in all the tests before. Instinctively, I tried to beat the test yet again, as though I was competing against that depressing downward slope.

It was a big mistake.

When Allison entered the testing room where I waited, I could see her struggle to maintain her professional distance.

"I am so sorry, Diane. I have no idea how you can hear so little actual sound and yet still manage to understand sentences."

She went over my chart, explaining that while I had clearly qualified for a cochlear on all the tests that indicated what I was hearing through beeps and buzzes, I had "failed" the test with sentences. By failed, she meant that I had "heard" just a tad too well.

How was that possible?

Apparently, my ears' inability to hear distinct sounds was augmented by my brain's instinctual habit of putting bits and pieces of information together. If I heard "kate" and another indistinct syllable, I intuitively figured out that the word must be "skateboard." After over a decade of listening to the exact same CD of compound words and short sentences, my guesses were often correct.

I walked out of the office crestfallen, barely able to look at Phil, whose expression, I was certain, was as bleak as mine. How could I not qualify as deaf? I could hardly hear anything, couldn't have a conversation as we walked to our car. The echoes in the parking garage would distort the barely perceptible words, making their meaning indecipherable.

Phil knew that trying to hear had become an exercise in futility for me. Unless I could find a place of complete quiet and stare intently at someone's face, someone who would not change topics without first telling me what we were talking about, someone who would speak slowly and clearly, I wouldn't understand a thing. Or, what seemed worse to me, I would hear just enough faint sound to leave me utterly confused. It was as if, just within reach of connection, my tentative hold on hearing slipped from my grasp.

I listened as one grabbing at air, falling into an abyss of silence.

Why hadn't I relaxed during the test and let the words float in one ear and out the other without working so hard to remember? Had I forgotten Janna's insistence, all those years ago, that I be honest about my hearing? Instead, I had shot myself in the foot by trying yet again to beat the test, by filling in what I couldn't hear with well-informed guesses.

We knew that a cochlear implant was my only hope for restored hearing, and insurance restrictions wouldn't allow me to be tested again for another year. There was nothing anyone could do except advise me to not try so hard next time.

That was a long year.

After being rejected as a candidate for an implant, I lived mostly inside my head, the strain of trying to make sense of what people were saying too difficult to keep up for more than a few minutes. Unable to enter the stream of human conversation, I longed more than ever to listen and talk and ask questions and disagree. I wanted to debate, to probe. I desperately wanted to enter into that unique fellowship of shared humor, to see the twinkle in another's eye and know why it was there.

I vividly remember the ache of not being able to call my daughter, then in her last year of college. I knew I was missing out on the delicious details of my girl's adventure. No one tried harder than Bekah to let me into her life, but the thick barrier of sounds that didn't make sense kept me from knowing what every mother wants to know, those secrets that leak out in unguarded moments. It's hard to catch those when every word must be articulated at full volume, then clarified using synonyms if I couldn't get it the first time. Not exactly an atmosphere that fostered intimacy.

I was lonely.

And yet, God was there—the One who stood by my side when the loneliness of my deafness isolated me from all others. His voice became clearer every day. A seventeenth century monk, Brother Lawrence, best expressed how I felt: "When outward business diverted him a little from the thought of God, a fresh remembrance coming from God invested his soul, and so inflamed and transported him that it was difficult for him to contain himself."[109]

God continued to invite me into a continual conversation with Himself. He drew me so near that I could virtually see the twinkle in His eye, catch His humor in shared delights.

Dallas Willard wrote, "Learning to hear God is much more about becoming comfortable in a continuing conversation and learning to constantly lean on the goodness and love of God, than it is about turning God into an ATM for advice, or treating the Bible as a crystal ball."[110]

Yes! In my alienation from human conversation, I was becoming more and more comfortable in that continuing conversation with the One who calls Himself Logos, the Word. This, as Brother Lawrence put it, is the key to practicing the presence of God—that moment-by-moment awareness that invites His kingdom into real time rather than relegating worship to the occasional tryst. In my loneliness, God was continuing to draw me into an intimacy with Him I had never known possible.

Could it be that God invites every one of us into that kind of intimacy?

My husband and son started a church that year. An offshoot of the church where Phil was on staff, Solid Rock was launched on Easter Sunday with a core team of one hundred and fifty people to help us get started. I itched to jump in and wrap myself around our people, longed to know each and every person who graced us with their presence. And I tried. But there's not a lot a woman can do when she can barely limp through even the most elementary of conversations.

So I walked the suburban neighborhoods near my house and simply talked to God about our venture. Up and down the hills, I passed houses and prayed. For blessing, for spiritual hunger, for desire to know God.

And I listened. Sometimes, as I was walking by a particular house, I sensed a sort of intensity of need. So I'd walk a little slower, pouring out petitions, syncing my heart with God's. I was propelled by the uncanny sense that what I was doing was vital. That my listening and my asking were somehow unlocking doors the enemy had fastened tight. One day, I stumbled on a story in the book of Daniel that convinced me I was right.

Daniel lived in desolate times. He was alone in his faith, or nearly so. Surrounded by people who neither knew God nor wanted Him, Daniel's heart ached with a burden to see God move. In his aloneness, Daniel cried out to God over and over for these people.

"Now, our God, hear the prayers and petitions of your servant. For your sake, Lord, look with favor on your desolate sanctuary. Give ear, our God, and hear; open your eyes and see the desolation of the city that bears your Name. We do not make requests of you because we are righteous, but because of your great mercy. Lord, listen! Lord, forgive! Lord, hear and act! For your sake, my God, do not delay, because your city and your people bear your Name."[111]

And God heard! While Daniel was praying and pleading for his people, undoubtedly wondering why God seemed silent, a war was raging in that unseen world the Bible refers to simply as the "heavenly realms."[112] For three full weeks, as Daniel prayed, an unnamed angel wrestled for control of that region against "the prince of the Persian kingdom."[113] Somehow, Daniel's prayers summoned the help of Michael, God's top agent, and the two angels asserted the power of God to put an end to the stranglehold the evil one held over that area.[114]

As I walked and listened and asked God to lift the stranglehold that has kept the Pacific Northwest one of the most unchurched regions of America, I began to get a growing sense that my contribution to our church plant might well be mysteriously imbedded in these rambling walks. As a nearly deaf woman, I couldn't *do* much, but I *could* talk to the One who is "able to do far more abundantly beyond all that we ask or think." [115]

So I did. For hours and hours and hours, I prayed my way past households of people I knew needed Jesus.

The church that started with a relatively small nucleus of worshipers now welcomes thousands every week. Traffic jams the road leading to the warehouse-turned-holy place where we hold services. Everywhere we go, we run into people who recognize Phil and eagerly share their stories of life-changing redemption.

How could I have doubted that God was using me in the obscurity of my silence? How could I have believed my disability made me inept for ministry?

I wonder sometimes while I'm listening to yet another story of someone inexplicably drawn to our church and subsequently to Jesus—*what if I hadn't?* What if I hadn't listened to that voice urging me out the door to slog through Oregon rain?

On Friday nights, I watched from the back wall of the church as my son's teaching helped turn over a thousand college-age people into passionate followers of Jesus. And as I leaned against the cold concrete, wishing I could understand what John Mark was saying, God's presence again enfolded me and assured me of my worth.

I knew I was needed—not for what I could do but for how I could pray.

My eyes scanning the backs of shaved and tattooed and bleached and dreadlocked heads, I asked God to open their hearts to hear. Watching the worship, seeing the way they leaned in to listen to the words my son was teaching, I listened to that voice and let Him lead me in how to pray. I knew parents were praying, could imagine a grandmother's prayers luring her offspring to this very spot. I felt as if I was partnering with people I didn't know in asking for His mercy to flood this place.

Could this be why I had failed the test?

Even as I was warmed by the sight of so many young men and women making the courageous choice to let go of the comfortable and go after God with abandon, I questioned my fear of cochlear surgery.

I wanted to hear my son. *I* wanted to embrace these people, to enter into their stories, to talk and listen and be a part of this family. And I wanted to hear my own family.

Remembering that Thanksgiving table—the dreadful sense of isolation, of being out of the loop, unable to experience the joy of relationship—I decided then and there to take whatever risks were required to get back into the circle of friendship and fellowship and family.

Watching was no longer enough. I wanted to hear again, and I'd do anything to be sure I could.

And so it was that I finally gave up trying to beat the hearing test. I flunked my next exam, with honors. Out of one hundred words read aloud to me, I correctly repeated back five—with the amplification of the biggest, strongest hearing aids on the market.

I was officially deaf.

A few months later, I lay swathed in hospital blankets, trundling down a corridor, looking into the faces of the medical team who would try to make me hear again. I knew enough to be afraid. And I knew enough to be determined. I sensed God's blessing, but no promises. Just the conviction that by doing the next thing, the dreaded thing, I was not passively resigning myself to the disconnection of deafness. Nearly eighteen years since I began to lose my hearing, it was my turn, my only chance at hearing.

A last-ditch attempt to come back into the world of sound.

I knew everything that could go wrong: blood clots in an area of the head that bleeds copiously, meningitis, balance difficulties, permanent numbness, incessant tinnitus—as well as the complications inherent in any surgery. But what worried me most were all those papers I had to sign acknowledging that I knew how close the surgeon would be cutting to the facial nerve that controls the movement of cheeks and lips and eyelid. I pictured my mouth drooped to one side, saliva dripping unfelt down my chin, a lopsided smile with nothing cute about it. I imagined looking into a mirror, repulsed by the grimace that hid my smile. Would it be worth it?

A highly qualified technician would be standing right next to me during the surgery, monitoring the temperature of that delicate facial nerve, watching that it didn't overheat from the friction caused by the drilling. She would help the surgeon know when he was getting too close, when the nerve was lighting up and screaming to be left alone. I knew my surgeon was one of the best in the world, and I was being asked to trust him, to believe in his skill, in his record, in his passion to help people hear. But I had to sign a waiver just in case. Because, as good as he was, he wasn't infallible.

Several hours later, I woke to the insistent nudges of the recovery room nurse. She cupped the side of my face with her warm hand, telling me with her eyes what I could not hear. I was okay, the procedure had gone well. Prior to the surgery, this woman had told me she'd be praying for me, the love of God radiating from her beautifully lined face.

An angel in human skin.

She'd come in that morning and recognized my name on the whiteboard over the nurse's station. She knew about the church we'd planted the year before, knew that her church had helped, and knew that she'd been sent that morning to care for me. While I was in surgery, she'd sought out Phil, giving him updates and listening to his concerns. By the time I was beginning to awaken, they were laughing like old friends, and I was being cared for like a queen.

I have learned to look for those kinds of encounters in this trek through a sometimes frightening world. In His kindness, God whispers assurance through His emissaries, and I have no doubt that my nurse that day was one of those.

So was Rebekah. She'd come to stay with me post-recovery, bringing her joyful, practical efficiency. Phil had been asked to lead the worship for a conference Luis Palau was speaking at on the Oregon coast. He took twelve-year-old Matthew with him, knowing that a quiet house combined with Bekah's ministrations would be the surest way for me to bounce back.

Fear lingered while my numb face figured out how to feel again. I'd been warned that the dizziness and loss of feeling in my face could last a while—weeks, or even months. And since one side of my face was swollen like a cyclops, we couldn't know how well the nerve would recover from the trauma of cutting and drilling so close.

But Bekah wouldn't let me dwell on doom. Instead, she set out to delight me with the treat of having her all to myself. We couldn't really talk, since my right ear was swollen beyond recognition, and I'd been advised not to attempt hearing aids in my other ear until my month of recovery was over and "hook-up" happened. But mothers and daughters on good footing don't need words to have fun, especially when the daughter's laugh reaches to her eyes, as Bekah's does. We read and I dozed and we turned on closed captioning to power through all the volumes of *Anne of Green Gables.*

I had an appointment scheduled one month post-surgery. It takes a month for the wound of cochlear implant surgery to heal enough for "hook-up" to the external unit that would conduct sound to the nerve. My facial swelling was receding nicely, with no obvious signs of trauma to the facial nerve. Only the faintest hint of residual numbness remained. The scar running up the back of my ear, skillfully hidden in the natural crease, covered the area where space for a coin-sized magnet had been carved out by the surgeon. The external unit had a corresponding magnet, which attached the receiver to my head. A plastic hook rested on the top of my ear, holding the batteries in place. Instead of the original purse-sized battery pack, now the rechargeable batteries would fit into a half-inch case hidden behind my earlobe.

Would it work?

Would I hear? And if so, how well? I walked into the appointment with a list of questions long enough to keep us there all day.

The initial activation of the cochlear produced some sound. I felt rather than heard the computer-generated noises, more like an uncontrollable twitch in my ear than recognizable sound. I tried to avoid looking at Phil's anxious face; I knew he felt my angst as if it was his own.

Gradually, I heard the beeps I was supposed to hear, responding with an ever more enthusiastic "yes" when Allison asked if I'd heard a specific tone. But I also heard sounds I couldn't recognize, so many sounds that by the time I'd left the appointment and was walking through the underground parking garage, my whole head reverberated with banging, clashing, deafening noise!

Allison's advice to me was clear: keep the cochlear on my head no matter how much the sounds rattled me. In time, she promised, my brain would become accustomed to the noise, sorting it all out. We hear with our brains more than with our ears, she explained. She instructed me not to avoid noise; the fastest, surest way to learn to hear again would be total immersion.

Somehow I had imagined a different sort of scenario when that cochlear got turned on.

I'd seen myself talking and listening and laughing and enjoying my people, not realizing all the other noises I'd have to sift through, like dogs barking. In those first weeks of hearing, it sounded like my drummer-husband's high-hats were being beat inside my head. The sound of my voice, something I hadn't heard in more years than I could remember, irritated me. I heard clicks every time I talked. The singers on the worship team sounded like Mickey Mouse.

I hated hearing!

Week after week, I went back to Allison, and I clung to her assurances. This was normal, she said. To be expected. What terrified me didn't alarm her in the least. That eighth bundle of nerves had atrophied, she explained. For so long it hadn't gotten anything but the weakest of signals, and now we were working it for all it was worth. Those beeps and whistles and Mickey Mouse sounds were actually the spasming of my nerves in response to all the noisiness of normal hearing.

One night after church, I was driving on the freeway toward home when out of nowhere, I heard a deafening roar. I frantically searched for a place to pull over. Heart pounding, I looked up to see if an airplane was crashing on my car. As I headed toward my exit, the sounds began to subside slightly. I detected a rhythm.

It was *rain.*

Rain was drumming a staccato rhythm on the roof of my car. I hadn't heard rain in so long, I'd forgotten that raindrops make noise. Beautiful, echoing plops and pitches danced like fairies on the wind. With the rain pouring on my roof and tears pouring down my cheeks, I lifted my face to the One who made the rain and cried with the purest joy.

From the side of the road, I texted Phil, "I hear rain!"

It was a turning point. The place where all I had gone through came together to become all I had hoped for.

I could hear.

CHAPTER 10

A Heart to Hear . . .

a story for you, too

A year later I sat at the same Thanksgiving table, with the same noisy people and a few more besides. I sat in the same place. Served the same food.

But this time nothing was the same.

Words floated into my cochlear processor, traveled easily down the spiral probe implanted in my ear, jolted that previously latent nerve into action, and registered in my brain. I laughed at the jokes, heard the punch lines. By this time I was even beginning to distinguish the distinctive differences in voices.

To hear again is a gift I celebrate every single day. It is a gift that has marked me, changed me at the very core of who I am.

Just a few weeks after the cochlear implant brought me back into the world of the hearing, I began to reach out of my shell of reserve. I began to initiate conversations, to ask questions.

For so long I had avoided talking to people who didn't know how to talk directly and distinctly to me. I had hidden behind a veil of reserve in order to protect myself from the intense embarrassment that came when I could not understand. Now I embraced people like a starving woman, eager to know them, to hear their stories, to enter into their lives. I couldn't get enough of this wonderful world of sound.

A miracle? Yes . . . and no.

Mine was a miracle that involved a whole lot of choosing and working and risk taking. Not *earning*, as I had thought, but *effort*.

To listen, to hear anything at all, I have to attach an uncomfortable computer to my head by matching the magnet to the bump just above my ear. As soon as I make that connection, my silent world goes loud. A swoosh of sound barrages the quiet. My brain scrambles to make sense of words and tones and volume and that jumble of racket that disrupts the restful place I was in just a moment ago.

Some days I put that jarring reality off as long as I can. Since I'm up before anyone else, I slip out of sleep wrapped in silence. I don't hear the rattle of the lid as I lift it off the can that holds the dog's food, nor does the sound of my creaking knees register as I walk down the stairs to make my tea. In the summer I open silent windows, in winter the fire I warm myself by makes no noise. Not a crackle, nor a pop, nothing.

And I like it that way. Really.

There is something so peaceful, so unhurried, when sound is muffled. The banging, the rattling, the clinking of glass, the noisiness caused by bumping up against all that happens every day—my deafness is a respite from all of that.

The irony is not lost on me—that I once feared the silence that is now my refuge.

As the sun begins to peek through uncovered windows and my world of relationships and responsibilities stirs, the time comes when I need to leave my cocoon of quiet. Deliberately, with a certain steadfastness of purpose, I open the box that holds my cochlear device, push the pulsing button that turns it on, brush my hair out of the way, and slide it into place.

And that's when the real work begins. For a deaf adult to break into the world of the hearing takes mammoth effort and immense determination. With my brain sorting through all those sounds, organizing, defining, and making sense of the noisiness, I am forced out of that place of silent listening into the rush of real life.

It took the better part of two years after the implant for my ears and brain to adapt to the incoming sound. That was a period of tweaking the computer, stretching my ability to process the auditory information that my brain had been bereft of for so long. While I can hear nearly everything now, my brain cannot always interpret the sound in a way that makes sense. I do not hear "naturally," but compared to hearing aids, a cochlear makes sounds so much sharper.

Sometimes, however, the device falls off or the batteries give out. Pretty awkward in social situations! I cannot understand, still, in crowded, noisy places. All that information collides on its way into my brain and sounds like one loud indistinguishable clamor.

The phone is still my enemy. I learned that I didn't dare make appointments after I missed a minor surgery, thinking I'd heard Wednesday when the receptionist had said Tuesday. Instead, I text when I can or depend on others to make the calls I can't.

I "read" movies through special glasses provided now by most movie theaters. The words glow in an eerie green on the far right corner of the lenses while my eyes dart back and forth between screen and the closed captioned words. Between what I can hear and what I see, I delight in the drama that once left me clueless.

Most of the time, music sounds terrible to me. A blaring clash of unpleasant, too-loud noises. I look around in church and know that I'm missing something vital, and yet I have learned to "sing" to the beat of the bass, to relish the words and feel the fellowship of the worshipers. My monotone blends with the beauty I cannot hear and I feel the awe.

But it's people I want to hear more than anything else.

The first time I realized I was understanding every word of a story my son was telling me from the backseat of the car, I started to cry in awed celebration.

Without the cochlear implant I would be relegated to a life of watching. I wouldn't hear the silly things children say or know why people are laughing. I couldn't navigate the grocery store or participate in a meeting or listen to a sermon. My speech would go back to sounding slurred, with the too-rounded vowels dominating the way I talk when I can't hear the sounds my mouth makes. I don't miss that at all.

But all this making sense of sounds can be exhausting. And some days I dread doing it. I get lazy, content to drift alone, without interaction and all the conflict and confusion that results from trying to listen when I can't hear quite right.

That is what listening to God can be like.

Sometimes I just don't want to. It's too much work, too confusing, too much effort. There's always the fear that I won't hear. Or that I won't understand. That I'll open my Bible, turn to the part I've assigned myself to read, and hear nothing. Or the words won't make sense. Or worse, they will, and I won't want to do what they say.

Forgive? Again? But it isn't fair. Why does it always have to be me?

Confess? Repent? But I like doing life my way, it feels good, right. Why can't it be about me for a change?

Some days I just don't want to go that deep. I'd rather read the paper, watch the news, hear about the escapades of other people. Or sleep a little longer and rush for the door just in time to meet my day, hurriedly crossing each thing off my list.

I think many of us have become comfortable with not hearing God. To deliberately decide to cultivate a close connection with God is hard work.

It's not just about hearing how much He loves me and wants the best possible life for me. More often, He has tasks for me to do. Corrections to give. Adjustments in my attitude to make.

And while He pours mercy all over my mistakes, He also insists on making me aware when I've done wrong.

Just like putting on my cochlear device is all mixed up with wonders and work, so putting on a heart to hear God is a mixed bag of delight and discipline.

But it is this day in, day out decision to abide in Him that allows me to really know Him. When I hear Him every day, the cadence of His voice becomes familiar. I know the difference between the way He speaks and that accusing voice of the enemy or that excusing voice of my own self-deception.

To hear Him now is my greatest delight. Early every morning, before the world awakes, I meet Him in the quiet. I open my Bible, pick up my pen, and wait for words, inviting Him to speak to me, writing what I hear. I bring my honest hurts to Him, my hopes, my fears, all the angst I cannot handle on my own. I worship. I seek wisdom. I wait.

In that intimacy I know His nearness. I feel hope. I am safe.

I know better now, than to think that listening to God will free me from all my troubles. My story won't let me lose myself down that rock-strewn path again. And I don't carve out space to hear because I am disciplined, but because I want Him, all of Him.

I *need* God in a way I never knew I did before.

Knowing my story and the new song He had put in my mouth, a woman dear to me wanted to talk. She needed to be heard, to be understood, and perhaps most important—not *misunderstood.*

And so I listened long to the worries that roiled like a tumultuous sea within her soul. I asked careful questions, probing, uncovering, repeating back what I heard, reaching to understand. And then listened more.

All the while, I sensed the Spirit saying *"Shhh . . ."* to me.

"Do not offer advice. No, not that verse again—hush! Don't try to help this one you love, just listen—for Me."

So I did.

And what I heard as I listened—not for what I should say, not for what was wrong, but *for Him*—was the barest refrain echoing over and under her words, first faintly, then with greater intensity.

He was speaking to her!

She didn't know it yet, but I did. In her response to His whispers of conviction, her longing for freedom, the way she kept vacillating between feelings of angst and sureness of faith, I could hear her heart connecting to His. This one, this girl whose heart beats so like mine, whose wrestling sounded so like mine—was hearing Him.

And I wanted to stand up and shout—to dance, to weep and laugh and clap my hands in wonder that not only does He speak to me, but He speaks to this one too.

Isn't that why we worship?

Because God came near. And God stays near. And God draws us near.

I know what is ahead for this girl-woman I love.

At first she'll hear a whisper and not know what it means. She'll hunger. Thirst. She'll catch the faintest whiff of Him, that alluring fragrance that leaves a trail of His going.

Then she'll hear nothing and wonder why.

Something will go wrong. Big or small, it doesn't matter, just enough to slow her down, to cause her to look for Him again, to *want,* without knowing what it is she wants.

And the wanting will grow. The hunger will beckon. Her thirst will send her searching.

And I know this because that was me. A long time ago I thought I had it figured out, the formula for right living. Then my world fell apart. I heard the *D*-word, the unthinkable: deafness. In desperation I turned to God and pleaded as if my life depended on it—and in my mind, it did. I needed healing, and I needed hope for Him to step in to do what I knew He could and was sure He would.

And when He didn't . . . I raged and despaired. Even hated Him.

But there, right in that place, with not a shred of goodness, no hint of godliness, no hope of getting it right and climbing out on my own, He spoke to me.

I cannot explain exactly what happened that day in the cinder-block room where the elders prayed for me but I know for sure that He revealed something of Himself to me.

I know that He rescued me in that moment—from myself, from self-destruction, from Satan's up-till-then-successful-plan to separate me from the love of Christ.

I know that in that rescue I heard Him tell me that He wouldn't give me what I wanted, but that instead He would give me my heart's truest desire.

And I knew I had to choose.

I still do.

I choose to believe that God is good even though He didn't heal me. That when life goes wrong and I suffer, He is with me. I join with the prophet to sing, "He deals wondrously with us!"[116] even when the wonderful life I expected doesn't turn out the way I'd hoped.

I don't know your story. I don't know if you're a good girl trying too hard to be better, or if you're a mess-up wanting what you want and wanting it now. I don't know if you stopped caring long ago, or if you're teetering on the edge of an abyss, desperate to do whatever it takes to grab hold of happiness.

Maybe you'll close this book with a sigh and feel sadness for the roughly seventy million people the world over who cannot hear.

But far beyond that, I hope you hear in my story an echo of what I know He wants in yours. The same thing He wanted in David's story and Jacob's and Job's and Paul's and Sarah's.

What we all have in common is a desperate pull between the desire to live our own stories and God's desire that we be absorbed into His.

I pray that you will close this book and call out to God. That you will give credence to your hunger, pay attention to the thirst that has left you weaker than you knew.

I pray that you will have the audacity to wrestle for what your soul longs for. That you will struggle and contend and refuse to let go until you hear Him.

I pray that you will keep hanging on until His voice becomes recognizable, reliable, sure. That you will never again settle for the status-quo, duty-bound, good life.

May His whispers become so essential to your soul that you would go anywhere, let go of anyone, do anything to hear Him. And may you join with the Jacobs throughout history—women like me—in grabbing hold of God and insisting you will not let go until He blesses you.

Until you hear.

A Word of Thanks To . . .

Bill Jensen, for not giving up on me when I thought I couldn't do it.

Carolyn McCready, for making it possible—and for friendship.

Traci Mullins, for turning my scribbles into a story.

The rest of the Zondervan team: Harmony, Bridget, Tom, Bridgette, Curt, Tim, Kait . . . for creating beauty.

The Sistas, for endlessly praying me through my fears.

My girls, readers of my blog, for reminding me over and over how desperately you long to hear.

Dr. Gerry Breshears, for reading and correcting and commenting and encouraging. Your notes have explained to me what I needed to know.

My dad, for letting me be who I am. How I wish you could have lived long enough to read these words. I miss you every day.

My son John Mark, for cheering me on and urging me to *"Write what only you can write, Mom!"* You give me courage to just be me.

My daughter Beth, for formatting my long paragraphs into readable prose that sounds like me both in this book and on the blog. And for caring as much as I do for "*my girls.*"

My daughter Bekah, for that enchanting weekend in Victoria when you listened to my story for the first time, making me dig deeper into the raw parts, and for flying to Portland for two intense days of major surgery on my manuscript. You made this story what I couldn't.

My son Matt, for talking to me no matter hard it is, no matter how much time it takes for me to get it. Somehow you just seem to understand more than anybody how much I *need* to hear.

And lastly, my husband, for loving me no matter what, for leading me always closer to Jesus, for this wild adventure of partnering together to serve Him first.

Notes

1. John 14:15 NASB.

2. Genesis 16:2, paraphrased.

3. Genesis 16:5, paraphrased.

4. Dr. Gerry Bershears notes that the best meaning of this word is actually *wonderful*. *"Is anything too wonderful for the* Lord*?"*

5. Genesis 18:13–15 NLT. Dr. Gerry Bershears notes: "The tone in God's voice is a critical part. Is He angry? Disappointed? Compassionate? I think the last. Many think the first."

6. Dr. Gerry Bershears: "A key to this story is that she relied on God's promise and it did not happen. It is no wonder that she does not trust Him as she once did. He had every opportunity to come through in her old but still possible age. Now she is far past possibility and God has failed in His promise. And He never spoke to her to clarify. This has a major parallel to Gen. 15 where Abraham expresses his own 'why did You not keep Your promise?' When God renewed the promise, Abraham 'amended' Him and God counted/esteemed that trust to be righteousness. We wonder what Sarah's response was to God's renewal of the promise."

7. Lewis, C. S. *A Grief Observed.* (New York: Harper & Row, 1961), 17.

8. Job 7:11, 16; 10:1–3 NLT.

9. Ruth 1:20–21 NLT.

10. Psalm 38:21–22 NLT.

11. Psalm 28:1 NLT.

12. James 5:14–15 NLT.

13. The Scriptures speak of God dwelling in "unapproachable light," I Timothy 6:16.

14. Thank you to my daughter, Rebekah, who on a long weekend listening to my story, brought the incongruence of God's beautiful *NO* to my attention. I've been relishing it ever since.

15. Psalm 40:2 NLT.

16. Psalm 104:2 NLT. Also, what both Daniel (Daniel 7:9) and Paul (I Timothy 6:16) described as His throne of light.

17. Job 42:5 NLT.

18. Romans 12:2 in the NASB reads: "And do not be conformed to this world, but be transformed by the renewing of your mind, so that you may prove what *the will of God is, that which is good and acceptable and perfect*" (emphasis mine).

19. Matthew 1:18–25.

20. Luke 1:38 NASB.

21. Luke 10:42.

22. Mark 16:7–11, paraphrased.

23. Philippians 2:6–8 NLT

24. Romans 12:1 says: "Therefore, I urge you brothers and sisters, in view of God's mercy, to offer your bodies as a living sacrifice, holy and pleasing to God—this is your true and proper worship."

25. 2 Samuel 12:3 NLT.

26. Dr. Gerry Bershears notes: "His story pierced through the armor into David's hidden world of shame and guilt and it blew out in irrational anger against the rich man. The point is that stealing a sheep is hardly a death penalty crime. Nathan turned David's godly heart toward his own stuff." Just as God was gently turning my heart away from the false confidence of my good girl self-righteousness toward "my own stuff."

27. 2 Samuel 12:7–9 NLT.

28. 2 Samuel 12:13.

29. Psalm 51.

30. Psalm 51:6 ESV.

31. James 5:16.

32. Zodhiates, Spiros. *The Complete Word Study Dictionary: New Testament* (Chattanooga, TN: AMG Publishers, 2000).

33. I Peter 3:18, emphasis mine.

34. Thank you, Dr. Bershears, for reminding me that this is the resurrection that comes after the cross. That a woman as entitled and self-righteous as I was is brought near again to the God she scorned.

35. Once again, I am weaving my imagination through the facts of the story. Perhaps it is a chip on my own shoulder that causes me to see one on hers. Read it for yourself to sense her longing for the soul-deep satisfaction that had eluded her.

36. John 4:9 NASB.

37. John 4:10, 13–14 NLT.

38. See Paul's story in 2 Corinthians 12:1–10.

39. Psalm 18:16–17.

40. Psalm 18:20–24.

41. God says He "remembers that we are dust," (Psalm 103:14) and that He is "a priest who fully understands our suffering" (Hebrews 4:15, paraphrased).

42. Oatman, Johnson Jr. "Count Your Blessings," *Songs for Young People* (Chicago, IL: Edwin O. Excell, 1897).

43. Zodhiates, *The Complete Word Study Dictionary: New Testament*.

44. James 5:10–11, emphasis mine.

45. For more about "those who have persevered," take some time to study the stories of the heroes of the faith in Hebrews 11.

46. Luke 1:42–45.

47. John 19:25–27.

48. Luke 2:35: note Simeon's prophesy spoken to Mary and Joseph when Jesus was just a few days old.

49. Read the story in Genesis 12:10–20 and a second time in Genesis 20.

50. Read the story in Genesis 26:1–11.

51. Genesis 25:28.

52. Read the whole convoluted story starting in Genesis 25:19— Genesis 35.

53. Thomas, W. H. Griffith, *Genesis, A Devotional Commentary* (Grand Rapids, MI: Eerdmans Publishing Company, 1946), 255.

54. Genesis 31:38.

55. Genesis 29:17.

56. Walton, John H., Victor H. Matthews and Mark. W. Chavalas, *The IVP Bible Background Commentary: Old Testament* (Downers Grove, IL: 2000), 62.

57. Genesis 29:25.

58. Genesis 29:25–31.

59. Exodus 3:6, 15–16.

60. Leviticus 19:11.

61. Jacob means *he grasps the heel*, a Hebrew idiom for *he deceives*.

62. Genesis 31:26–28 NLT.

63. Genesis 32:26 KJV.

64. Thomas, *Genesis, A Devotional Commentary*, 304.

65. Buchanan, Mark, *The Rest Of God* (Nashville: Thomas Nelson, 2008), 108.

66. Which, in fact he did, along with a new name—one that would define and direct the rest of his life, and then live on to define his heritage. The name of what would someday be a nation. Israel.

67. Five times in this passage, the writer calls this mysterious being, "the man," but in the end he identifies himself as God (Gen. 28) as does Hosea 12:3–5.

68. Matthew 5:3.

69. Matthew 7:28.

70. Matthew 5:3 NLT.

71. Genesis 46:2–3.

72. Willard, Dallas, *Hearing God: Developing a Conversational Relationship with God, Expanded Edition* (Downers Grove, IL: InterVarsity Press 1984, 1993, 1999, 2012), 115.

73. Ibid.

74. Philippians 1:3–6 NIV. He included his own suffering in 4:11–14 "Not that I am speaking of being in need, for I have learned in whatever situation I am to be content. I know how to be brought low, and I know how to abound. In any and every circumstance, I have learned the secret of facing plenty and hunger, abundance and need. I can do all things through him who strengthens me. Yet it was kind of you to share my trouble" (ESV). Paul's sufferings were very real, as was the blessing he found in the midst of them.

75. I Thessalonians 1:2–4.

76. The rest of his prayer in Ephesians 3:14–21 (NLT) is just as insightful: "Then Christ will make his home in your hearts as you trust in him. Your roots will grow down into God's love and keep you strong. And may you have the power to understand, as all God's people should, how wide, how long, how high, and how deep his love is. May you experience the love of Christ, though it is too great to understand fully. Then you will be made complete with all the fullness of life

and power that comes from God. Now all glory to God, who is able, through his mighty power at work within us, to accomplish infinitely more than we might ask or think. Glory to him in the church and in Christ Jesus through all generations forever and ever! Amen".

77. Tozer, A. W., *The Pursuit of God* (Camp Hill, PA: Christian Publications, 1982, 1993), 19.

78. Colossians 1:9–11.

79. Genesis 16:13.

80. Psalm 116:1–2 NLT.

81. What we call the Old Testament.

82. Buchanan, *The Rest Of God*, 185.

83. Genesis 16; 21:8–20.

84. I Corinthians 10:11–12 NLT.

85. I Peter 3:6 NASB.

86. Psalm 40.

87. Buchanan, *The Rest Of God*, 188.

88. Psalm 46:10.

89. Matthew 11:28–30 NASB.

90. Psalm 23.

91. Isaiah 55:3 NLT.

92. Hosea 1:1.

93. Hosea 1:2.

94. Hosea 1:3–9.

95. Hosea 2:5.

96. Hosea 2:14.

97. Hosea 6:3 NASB.

98. Hosea 2:14.

99. Romans 1:20.

100. John 8:12 NASB.

101. I first heard the term, "communication disorder" when I was invited to share my story for a class of speech pathology and audiology majors at Portland State University. What an apt description of how the loss of this vital sense brings disorder to my ability to communicate.

102. Tozer, *The Pursuit of God*, 1.

103. Matthew 9:1–8.

104. Mark 2:3–12.

105. Luke 5:18–26.

106. Matthew 9:2, 6.

107. Matthew 9:8.

108. Psalm 46:10.

109. Brother Lawrence, *The Practice of the Presence of God* (Peabody, MA: Hendrickson Publishers, 2004), 14.

110. Willard, *Hearing God: Developing a Conversational Relationship with God*, 10.

111. Daniel 9:17–19.

112. Ephesians 2:6.

113. Daniel 10:13.

114. Daniel 10:20—11:1.

115. Ephesians 3:20 NASB.

116. Joel 2:26, paraphrased.

More from Diane . . .

I live in a small cottage in the woods of the Northwest. In the back is a smaller cabin where I go every morning to listen and study and read and write.

A couple of times a week, I tidy up my scribbles and post them on my blog at www.hespeaksinthesilence.com.

That is where I write about normal life with all its quandaries, worries, and treasures. It is also where I invite friends to listen in on what I hear in the quiet of my world.

I have posted a small groups discussion guide of *He Speaks in the Silence: Finding Intimacy with God by Learning to Listen.*

Might you join me there?

My husband and I also lead a ministry called INTENTIONAL: Raising Passionate Jesus Followers. We teach and share stories together about how to ignite in your child a heart that beats for God. We believe it is God's first and foremost plan to reach the world with His love by making disciples of our own children. If you would be interested in knowing more about our conferences, please contact Phil Comer through the website www. intentionalparents.org.

If you would be interested in having me speak at your retreat or conference, please go to my website and find the *Contact Me* tab. It brings me great joy to share my story and what I am learning with women who want more.